Frugal One Pot Meals

Zero Waste Recipes to Save You Time and Money

Amber Smoak

Table of Contents

Introduction

"Those who think they have no time for healthy eating will sooner or later have to find time for illness."

-Edward Stanley

Do you want to eat healthily but don't want to burn a hole in your pocket? Do you love to cook but hate the thought of cleaning up a sink full of utensils later? Do you love the idea of home-cooked meals but don't want to spend too much time or money on them? Are you always in a hurry and tired of thinking about what your next meal is? What if you can enjoy delicious and healthy home-cooked meals using a single pot? Yes, you read it right. If this idea appeals to you, this is the perfect book for you.

When it comes to cooking, most of us use a variety of appliances and equipment. A conventional meal usually involves a variety of utensils and appliances. Even those who love cooking shy away from it because of all the clearing involved. Also, there will be days when we don't have the time or energy left to cook at home. Well, on all such days or even in general, shifting to one pot meals is a wonderful idea. The different kitchen appliances or equipment that can be used include a skillet or sauté pan, an instant pot or a slow cooker, and a roasting pan or baking dish. If you have any or all of these at home, you can use them to whip up delicious home-cooked meals within no time.

The world we live in is dominated by the notion of convenience. Walk into any supermarket and you will be bombarded with hundreds of food choices. However, seldom are they healthy. Instead of relying on take-out, ready-to-cook meals, or any other options along these lines, it's better to cook at home. Unfortunately, most believe that cooking and eating healthily is expensive and time-consuming. Well, you don't always need the most expensive ingredients to cook flavorful and healthy meals. Instead, it's about a little creativity. Nutrition is important and it can be done on a budget. After all, unless you provide your body with all the nutrients it needs, it cannot function effectively and efficiently. Improper nutrition can effectively get in the way of your dreams and goals. Therefore, focusing on that is needed. Are you wondering how you can do all this? If yes, look no further because this book has got your back.

In this book, you will discover recipes that are not only easy to cook but can be cooked within a budget as well. You don't have to burn a hole in your pocket because you want to eat healthy and delicious meals at home. You don't have to waste your time or hard-earned money doing this. All the recipes given in this book can be cooked within a tight budget. Also, they can all be cooked using a single pot. Forget about washing a sink full of utensils, cutlery and cooking appliances and vessels. Instead, you simply need one single pot to do it all. Whether it is a slow cooker or an instant pot, a conventional skillet, or a baking dish, you simply need one of these things to whip up tasty food within no time! All the recipes given in this book are divided into different categories. You will find a variety of recipes that can be cooked by using the skillet or sauté pan, slow cooker, and a roasting pan or baking dish. Also, the recipes are further divided into breakfast, lunch, dinner, and dessert categories for each of these means of cooking.

All that you need to do is simply select the different recipes that strike your fancy and gather the required ingredients. Once everything is in place, just follow the simple steps discussed in the recipe, and voila, a meal is ready within no time! It's not just the time spent cooking, but the time spent cleaning reduces as well. This coupled with a little meal prepping and planning, and batch cooking will make your life even easier. Cooking has never been this simple before. The only thing you must do is keep an open mind and let your creativity run wild. Once you get the hang of single-pot meals, you will not want to go back to any other method of cooking.

So, are you eager to get started? If yes, there's no time like the present to begin!

Chapter 1:

Getting Started With One Pot Meals

A common notion most have is that cooking is associated with spending hours together in the kitchen preparing cooking and cleaning up. Well, all this is about to change once you get into the groove of cooking one pot meals. Before discovering all the delicious and nutritious recipes in this book, let's learn a little about why these meals will become your best friend, how easy it is to eat on a budget, and a little about zero-waste cooking, and meal planning.

Why Are One Pot Meals Your Friend?

So, what are one pot meals? As the name suggests, it simply refers to the act of cooking everything in a single pot. It can be a slow cooker or an instant pot, a sauté pan or a skillet, or a baking dish or tray. If you have any or all of these things at home, you are in for a treat. Cooking one pot meals are not only time-saving but extremely simple too. Imagine, you simply need to toss all the ingredients into a single pot and let it do the rest of the work for you. Forget about constantly shifting between multiple pots and pans. Instead, you simply need one of these things and home-cooked meals will be ready within no time.

One of its most obvious benefits is that it drastically reduces the cooking time. All the time saved can be redirected toward anything you want to do. It's entirely up to you what you want to do with the extra time. Also, one pot meals are extremely simple to prepare. You will also only have a single pot to clean up which makes cooking itself extremely simple.

These meals also ensure that you are getting all the nutrients you require from a single dish or pan. This makes it easier to incorporate a variety of ingredients into whatever recipe you are cooking. Since all the ingredients are cooked in the same pot and you're not transferring them, the nutrients released are also trapped in there. This means the meals are automatically fortified with all the nutrients and nothing is lost. Most one pot recipes require the ingredients to be smart, roasted, or slow-cooked. This means the meals are automatically more flavorful. It's also a great way to introduce new ingredients, especially if you have picky eaters at home. Another benefit of one pot cooking is it makes for ideal leftovers. For instance, a pan of roasted chicken from one night can be turned into a salad, sandwich filling, or even a quick side dish for the next day.

A Little About Meal Prepping, Planning, and Batch Cooking

"What's for dinner?" This is one question that most of us dread thinking about, especially at the end of a tiring or hectic day. There will be days when you barely have any energy to cook or days when you don't feel like cooking. On all such days, ready-to-eat meals and takeout become the go-to options. Unfortunately, these options are not just expensive but filled with foods devoid of important nutrients. The only way to reverse this is by cooking at home. However, does the thought of cooking multiple meals every day for the entire week sound extremely stressful, tiring, or overwhelming? Well, all this is about to change. Once you get into the groove of meal planning and prepping, and batch cooking, you will realize how simple cooking is.

Imagine this situation, after a tiring day at work you come home. You have a portion of grilled chicken and pasta sauce in the fridge. Simply reheat these ingredients along with some pasta and you can dig into a 100% home-cooked meal that is healthy and simple! This is how all your meals will be with a little planning and preparation.

Meal Planning

As the name suggests, meal planning refers to deciding what you want to eat or all the meals you wish to eat within a week. This is a great way of sticking to a budget while keeping your nutritional goals in mind. Meal plans can be designed with a specific outcome in mind such as improving your overall health or even losing weight. Whatever it is, create a meal plan that works well for you. Once you know what you are eating, you'll need to shop for the required ingredients. A meal plan is the first step toward reducing food wastage. When you know what to cook and how much you will need, you can buy the groceries accordingly. Always remember that money saved is money earned.

Meal Prepping

Once the meal plan is in place, the next step is meal prepping. It refers to the concept of preparing dishes or even an entire meal ahead of schedule. This is especially helpful for busy individuals and helps save a lot of your time, money, and effort. Having a couple of prepared meals on hand is a great way to regulate the portion size while achieving your nutrition goals. Also, when all or most of the prep is already in place, time spent in the kitchen is further reduced.

Batch Cooking

There are different ways to meal prep. Some of the most popular techniques involve individually portioning the ingredients, prepping the ingredients required for specific meals, preparing the meals ahead and freezing them, and batch cooking. Batch cooking refers to preparing large batches of a specific recipe and then dividing it into individual portions that are saved for later. For instance, if there is a specific recipe that you love or know your family enjoys, make a large batch of it and freeze it for later. Whether it's a pasta sauce, curry, soup, stew, or anything else along these lines, make a big batch and freeze it. These things will come in handy, especially when you don't have any time or energy to cook but want to dig into home-cooked meals.

There are four simple steps to be followed to start batch cooking. The first step is to schedule a specific time to cook. The second step is to plan ahead what you wish to do during the batch cooking session. The third step is to gather the required groceries. And the fourth and final step to prep and cook. Unless you said some time aside to do this, chances are you will not get into the habit.

Once you have dedicated specific time, plan what you wish to do during that session. For instance, once you are aware of the meal plan for the week, look at all the different components or any preparation that can be done ahead. Whether it is cleaning and cutting vegetables, portioning ingredients for each of the recipes you wish to cook or even simply cooking a specific recipe, make a note of hurtful so once you know what you have to do, you can make the most of the time available.

After this, don't forget to gather the required groceries so that when you actually need to start speaking you don't have to waste any time searching for the ingredients. after all those commands simply start cooking and prepping. However, don't forget to properly store whatever you have cooked and crabbed filter but not, the effort time and the money spent doing this will go to waste.

Tips to Get Started

Take some time, go through all the recipes given in this book, and make a list of recipes that you wish to try or want to eat. Once you have an idea of all that you will be eating in a given week, select the meal prep method of your choice. This can be a combination of the methods mentioned above depending on your lifestyle as well as nutrition goals. For instance, you can include batch cooking along with individually portioning different ingredients for the meals you wish to cook. You can also precook an entire meal or certain ingredients. Doing all this will make it easier to put a meal together on a busy day.

After this, you'll need to stick to a schedule. Meal planning and prepping is not something you can do in 5-10 minutes. Instead, it takes a couple of hours. However, think of this as an investment in your health. Spend 3-4 hours over the weekend or on any day you have some time, plan the meals, and do the prep needed. Stick to this prepping schedule and cooking will become a breeze.

You will need to be mindful of the number of meals you wish to cook at home. If you are being fairly realistic, there will be days when you want to go out or eat out. Therefore, prep and plan such that you take into consideration any of the days when you will not be eating at home. This is a great way to reduce food wastage and avoid spending on ingredients that you will not use.

While starting, it's better to stick to simple recipes. This is where all the recipes in this book will come in handy. You will need to plan such that a variety of recipes are included so the meals do not become boring. If they become boring, even sticking to the schedule becomes difficult.

Before you head to the grocery store, ensure that you have a list on hand. The list must include only the items you need and, in the portions, or quantities that are needed and no more. Doing this regularly will help stick to a food budget and make you more aware of the food choices you are making. Whether you are purchasing the ingredients from a local grocery store or supermarket or ordering online, a list helps reduce the time and money spent on groceries. Also, before you decide to go shopping, take a stock of all the ingredients you have on hand. Look for means to utilize the ones you have at home before buying more. After all, you need to focus on zero-waste cooking.

While meal planning and prepping, look for recipes that have overlapping ingredients or steps. Plan the meal such that you can repurpose any of the leftovers and food isn't wasted. Leftovers are also great for busy days. That said, leave a little room for flexibility in your meal planning schedule. If it becomes too restrictive, the motivation to stick to it reduces. It is okay if you don't stick to the meal schedule once in a while. Instead of wasting the leftovers, get a little creative. Today's leftovers can become tomorrow's meal.

Finally, the most important aspect of meal planning, prepping, and batch cooking is to properly store the meals. If you are storing fully cooked meals, then you'll need to opt for the right cooling methods as well as appropriate containers. Plan your meal such that you end up utilizing the cooked food within 3-4 days or a week at the most.

Reducing the Time Spent Cooking

It will take some time to get into the groove of meal planning and prepping. However, this is a wonderful lifelong habit that will automatically reduce your time spent cooking. This coupled with batch cooking further reduces the time spent in the kitchen. While meal planning, reducing the time spent in the kitchen is one thing that you need to focus on. Here are some simple suggestions that will come in handy to streamline the process of meal prepping, planning, and cooking.

You should always start with a constant schedule. Meal prepping works incredibly well when you have a schedule or a routine in place. It's not just about having a schedule but you should also follow it too. This schedule will tell you when to shop for groceries, start meal planning, and prepping as needed. For instance, Sunday mornings might be reserved for grocery shopping. Similarly, you can select Monday evenings for preparing lunch for the rest of the week. When specific time is allocated for these activities out of your schedule, decision making is simplified. Also, you can plan the rest of the week around this.

If you want to become more efficient in the kitchen, then you need to learn to select the right combination of recipes. If you are selecting too many recipes that you want to cook at once or the recipe involves different components to be cooked separately, it doesn't make much sense. Apart from increasing the time spent in the kitchen, cleaning up also becomes difficult. Instead, opt for the simple and delicious one pot recipes given in this book. All the recipes can be cooked using a single appliance. Select the recipes such that they have certain overlapping ingredients or components. For instance, the recipes you select might have similar vegetables or protein in them. So the protein or the vegetables can be prepped accordingly. If you need diced or cubed vegetables for a recipe look for other recipes that use them too. This makes preparing the vegetables easy. Once all the ingredients are prepped, you simply need to toss them into the pot and let it all cook together.

Easy Ways to Eat Healthier on a Budget

When you think about eating healthily, images of expensive and exotic ingredients and small portions pop into your mind. However, this is not what healthy eating is all about. Instead, it is about becoming conscious of the quality and quantity you consume. You can easily revamp your grocery cart without burning a hole in your pocket. The first thing you must focus on is strategizing and creating a budget that you want to adhere to. After this, ensure that your kitchen is stocked with the required staples to minimize food wastage. If you want to start eating healthily on a budget, here are some tips you can use.

Inexpensive Cuts of Meat

Expensive cuts of meat taste good. You don't have to keep splurging on them all the time. Instead, even cheap cuts of meat can taste extremely delicious, provided you know how to cook them properly. Slow cooking is the best way to make the most out of a cheap cut of meat. Tougher cuts such as stew meat, pork shoulder, or even beef chuck (neck and shoulder) are quite cheap when compared to the other cuts such as tenderloin. Also, the former is ideal for one pot meals.

Seasonal Produce

As much as possible, opt for in-season vegetables and fruits. They are not only healthy and tasty but are cheaper too. Whatever is in season, add it to your menu. In fact, plan meals such that it incorporates more seasonal vegetables and produce. Also, if there are any specific seasonal fruits or vegetables you enjoy or your family likes, plan to store them in the freezer. Buying seasonal produce and freezing it for later is a great way to cut down on the grocery bill too.

Preserved Fruits and Veggies

You don't have to shy away from frozen produce. Whether it's frozen fruits or vegetables, they're not only less expensive than their fresh counterparts but are equally nutritious. Frozen produce is usually picked at a time when it is at its peak freshness and then frozen. You simply need to be a little creative to add all these ingredients to any of the meals you wish to cook. For instance, frozen peas and vegetables can be easily incorporated into stews, curries, and even soups. This reduces the time spent cleaning and cutting the produce along with their cooking time. Similarly, you can use canned vegetables, fruits, and other ingredients. Purchasing preserved foods in bulk; especially the frozen or canned varieties are quite economical. For instance, making a batch of homemade chili becomes extremely simple if you have a can of beans on hand.

Avoid Ready-Made Treats

Another great way to eat healthily while adhering to a budget is by skipping all ready-made treats that are deemed healthy. Instead of purchasing the so-called healthy foods, try to cook at home as much as possible. It's not only cheaper but is more nutritious too. After all, when you cook at home, you have complete control over the quality of ingredients used along with the quantity. This reduces food wastage, which in turn cuts down on your grocery bills.

Use the Freezer

Try to make the most of the freezer space available. You can use it to stock up on fresh produce and cut down on food wastage as well. Have you ever thrown bags of spinach because they were wilted or dry after lying dormant in the fridge for a couple of days or even weeks? Well, you no longer have to worry about such food wastage if you simply put it in freezer-friendly bags and store it in the freezer. Whatever it is, it can be stored in the freezer provided you do it probably.

Apart from all the suggestions mentioned until now, stick to the recipes given in this book. The recipes are not only healthy but can be cooked on a budget too! Feel free to experiment with different flavor combinations and don't hesitate to replace ingredients as per your tastes and preferences.

All Things Zero—Waste

Cooking and eating delicious meals can make anyone feel good. When such meals are shared with your loved ones, the entire experience is automatically elevated. However, a lot of waste is created in the production and preparation of food. This is one of the greatest challenges humanity is facing in terms of the sustainability of the existing food system. The good news is that we all have a choice when it comes to leading more sustainable lifestyles and this is where the concept of zero-wastage steps into the picture.

Zero-waste cooking is pretty much what it sounds like. It's about leaving as little waste as you possibly can while cooking and eating. It is based on the simple concept of reducing, reusing, and recycling. It means, cutting down on unnecessary ingredients, reusing whatever is available instead of throwing it, and recycling the kitchen waste and leftovers into compost whenever possible. These are just some of the few steps you can take to maintain a zero-waste household.

By shifting to a zero-waste cooking policy, you can reduce food wastage, reduce the dependence on plastics and packaging, and improve environmental health. This is also a great way to focus on consuming nutritional meals that are delicious and sustainable for everyone involved. Here are some simple steps to get started with zero-waste cooking.

Start With Meal Planning

The most straightforward means to reducing food wastage and keeping a zero-waste kitchen is to plan your meals. While planning, consider the perishable foods available, any bulk purchases that can be made, and how the same ingredient can be used across different recipes. You should also consider the serving sizes and how long any of the leftovers can be safely stored.

Instead of eating out and increasing food wastage, it is better to cook at home. This is where all the different recipes given in this book will come in handy. Eating out or ordering food is not only expensive but is seldom healthy when compared to home cooking. The good news is that the different meals in this book can be cooked on a tight budget while reducing food wastage. Get a little creative and try to repurpose and reuse any of the leftovers. This is where meal planning and prepping come into the picture. Apart from this, learn to preserve what's cooked and the ingredients too. Whether it is freezing, canning, pickling, or dehydrating, go ahead and do it.

Storage Options

No discussion about zero-waste cooking and meal prepping is complete without considering storage options. One of the best ways to store anything or increase the shelf-life of a cooked or uncooked ingredient is to store it in the freezer. If you have sufficient freezer space or an additional freezer, it is precious real estate in terms of freezing food. When it comes to freezing, the food must be wrapped and sealed tightly in freezer-friendly bags and similar airtight containers and bags. Once you store them properly, the ingredients can be simply reheated as and when the need arises. Don't try to refreeze a thawed ingredient. When stored properly, most cooked food is safe for a month or two. On the other hand, uncooked meat, poultry, and seafood can be frozen safely for up to 4 months. Similarly, even veggies and fruits can be safely stored in the freezer for months together.

While storing, ensure the freezer temperature is at 0°F or lower while the refrigerator is maintained at 40°F for storing food. Always cool the food quickly before placing it in the refrigerator or the freezer. Don't forget to label the foods stored and keep a list handy so you don't forget what's stored.

Investing in the right containers is important to store the food or ingredients properly. For instance, placing a glass container in the freezer is a terrible idea. It will not only damage the container but the food in it will be wasted too. On the other hand, freezer-safe containers and bags are the ideal choice. Apart from this, use airtight containers for storing ready-to-cook ingredients such as vegetables and fruits. Whether it is a stainless steel container or a reusable silicone bag, place the ingredients in it and keep it in the refrigerator to prolong its shelf life. Similarly, purchasing a couple of BPA-free microwavable containers is a good idea too. If you have batch cooked anything and you know you will be utilizing it within the next 3-4 days, then storing in such microwave-proof containers makes it easy to reheat or thaw.

If you practice the art of zero-waste cooking, you can significantly cut down on food bills and food wastage. However, practice hygiene while preserving food. This is also a great means to store any seasonal ingredients.

Chapter 2:

Skillet and Sauté Pan Recipes

Breakfast

Potatta

Serves: 3

Ingredients:

¼ cup slaw mix

2 green onions, sliced

Coarse salt to taste

4 ounces sour cream

Freshly ground pepper to taste

2 ounces Parmesan cheese or Swiss cheese, shredded

¼ cup chopped red bell pepper

8 ounces potatoes, quartered, cooked, chilled

5 large eggs

¼ cup chopped herbs of your choice

Directions:

Pour ½ tablespoon of oil into a heavy bottomed skillet and let it heat over medium heat. When the oil is hot, add onion, bell pepper, and slaw mix and stir.

Cook for 3–4 minutes stirring often. Add the potatoes and stir. Cook for a few minutes until light brown. Add salt and pepper to taste.

Crack eggs into a bowl. Beat the eggs well. Add half the sour cream, half the cheese, herbs, pepper, and salt and stir until well combined.

Spoon the egg mixture into the skillet, over the potatoes. Shake the skillet to spread the egg mixture. Do not stir. Cover the skillet with a lid.

Let it cook on medium-low heat for about 5 minutes or until the egg mixture is nearly set but not fully set.

Scatter remaining cheese on top. Cover and continue cooking until the egg sets, and is golden brown around the edges.

Turn off the heat. Cut into wedges. Place the wedges on individual serving plates. Drizzle remaining sour cream on top and serve.

Rice Porridge

Serves: 2

Ingredients:

<u>For the porridge:</u>

½ teaspoon pure vanilla extract

1 ½ cups leftover cooked brown rice or white rice

2 tablespoons coconut sugar or brown sugar

1 cup milk of your choice

1 tablespoon raisins

½ teaspoon ground cinnamon

1 tablespoon golden flaxseed meal

A pinch salt

<u>Serving options:</u>

¼ cup chopped almonds, toasted

2 teaspoons chia seeds

Pomegranate arils

2 tablespoons shredded coconut

Cacao nibs

Directions:

Add rice, vanilla, sugar, milk, raisins, cinnamon, flaxseed meal, and salt into a heavy bottomed skillet and stir. Place the skillet over medium heat.

Stir occasionally until thick or as per your preference. Remove from the heat.

Serve in bowls with any of the suggested serving options.

Country Breakfast Skillet

Serves: 2–3

Ingredients:

3 slices bacon, chopped into 2 inch pieces

1 small onion, finely chopped

¼ cup shredded sharp cheddar cheese

Salt to taste

⅛ cup chopped green bell pepper

3 cups cooked, cubed, potatoes

3 large eggs, lightly beaten

Pepper to taste

Directions:

Place a heavy skillet over medium heat. Add bacon and cook until crisp.

Take out the bacon with a slotted spoon and place on a plate lined with paper towels.

When bacon cools, crumble into smaller pieces.

Retain about 1 ½ to 2 tablespoons of the bacon fat in the skillet and drain off the remaining.

Increase the heat to medium-high heat. When the pan is hot, add onion, bell pepper, and potatoes and mix well. Stir occasionally until the potatoes are brown.

Add cheese all over the ingredients and mix well. Pour eggs all over the vegetables. Stir lightly. Cook until the eggs are set.

Sprinkle salt and pepper on top. Garnish with bacon and serve right away.

Breakfast Skillet With Steak and Eggs

Serves: 3

Ingredients:

½ pound flat iron steak

1 ¼ teaspoons House seasoning blend or any other seasonings of your choice

½ cup chopped bell pepper

3 large eggs

½ tablespoon olive oil

½ onion, chopped

10 ounces frozen shredded hash brown potatoes, defrosted

Salt to taste

Directions:

Pour oil into a skillet and let it heat over medium heat.

Sprinkle half of the seasoning blend on either side of the steak and slice it into about ½ inch thick slices.

Place steak slices in the skillet and cook for about 2 minutes. Flip sides and scatter onions and bell pepper in the skillet. Cook until the vegetables are tender.

Add hash browns and remaining seasoning into the skillet and mix well. Do not stir for about 7–8 minutes, or until the underside is golden brown.

Mix well. Now make three cavities in the mixture, at different spots. Crack an egg into each cavity. Turn down the heat to low heat and cook covered until the eggs and potatoes are cooked.

Orange Infused Steel Cut Oats

Serves: 2

Ingredients:

1 tablespoon butter

1 cup water

1 cup milk

1 tablespoon orange zest

¼ teaspoon vanilla extract

½ tablespoon maple syrup

¼ cup orange juice

¼ cup dried cranberries

½ cup steel cut oats

A pinch salt

Directions:

Add butter into a skillet and place the skillet over medium-low heat. When butter melts, add water, milk, orange zest, vanilla, maple syrup, steel cut oats, and salt and stir.

Cook covered for about 15 minutes or until the oats are cooked. If the oats are not cooked, and there is no liquid left in the skillet, feel free to add some more water or milk. Once the oats are cooked, turn off the heat.

Add cranberries and orange juice, stir and serve immediately.

Chocolate Steel Cut Oats

Serves: 2

Ingredients:

½ cup steel cut oats

1 ½ tablespoons cocoa

2 small bananas, mashed

1 ¾ cups water or milk of your choice (you can use a combination of milk and water)

Directions:

Place mashed banana, cocoa powder, and oats in a skillet. Pour milk and stir. Place the skillet over medium-low heat.

If the oats are not cooked, and there is no liquid left in the skillet, feel free to add some more water or milk. Once the oats are cooked, turn off the heat.

Stir well and serve.

Beefy Huevos Rancheros

Serves: 3

Ingredients:

½ pound lean ground beef (90% lean)

1 can (14.5 ounces) diced tomatoes

¼ cup liquid from the can of diced tomatoes

½ can (from a 4 ounce can) chopped green chilies

3 large eggs

3 tablespoons shredded cheddar cheese

½ small onion, minced

½ cup frozen corn

¼ teaspoon salt or to taste

Pepper to taste

3 flour tortillas, warmed

To serve: Optional

Guacamole

Low-fat sour cream

Sliced green onions

Directions:

Place a cast-iron or heavy skillet over medium heat. Add onion and beef and cook until the meat is not pink anymore. As you stir, break the meat into crumbles. Drain off all the excess fat from the pan.

Add tomatoes and its liquid, corn, salt, and chilies and mix well.

Let it start simmering.

Now make three cavities in the mixture, at different spots. Crack an egg into each cavity. Turn down the heat to low heat and cook covered until the eggs are cooked as per your preference.

Top with cheese and serve over tortillas with suggested serving options.

Lunch

Cheeseburger Macaroni Skillet

Serves: 3

Ingredients:

½ pound ground beef

½ tablespoon paprika

¾ teaspoon onion powder

½ teaspoon sugar

1 cup hot water

1 cup dry cavatappi or macaroni pasta

¾ teaspoon garlic powder

¾ teaspoon salt

¼ teaspoon black pepper

¾ cup milk

1 cup grated cheddar cheese

½ tablespoon cornstarch

Chopped parsley to garnish

Directions:

Add beef into a skillet and place it over medium-high heat. Cook until the meat is not pink anymore. As you stir, crumble the meat. Discard any extra cooked fat from the pan.

Combine paprika, cornstarch, garlic powder, salt, pepper, onion powder and sugar in a bowl and sprinkle this mixture all over the beef. Mix until well combined.

Stir in pasta, milk, and hot water. When the mixture starts boiling, turn down the heat and cook covered until the pasta is cooked.

Scatter cheese all over and mix well. Turn off the heat and let it sit covered for about 5–8 minutes.

Sprinkle parsley on top and serve.

Biscuit Chicken Pot Pie

Serves: 3

Ingredients:

½ tablespoon olive oil

½ cup chopped onion

1 celery stalk, diced

1 clove garlic, peeled, minced

½ teaspoon cracked pepper

2 cups chicken stock

½ pound chicken breast, diced

⅛ cup finely chopped parsley

1 small egg, beaten lightly

½ tablespoon butter

1 large carrot, diced

½ teaspoon dried thyme

Salt to taste

2 tablespoons all-purpose flour

2 tablespoons half and half

½ cup frozen peas

3 refrigerated biscuits

Directions:

Set the temperature of the oven to 350° F and preheat the oven.

Pour oil into an ovenproof skillet and let it heat over medium heat. Add butter and when butter melts, stir in the carrots, onion, and celery. When the vegetables are slightly tender, stir in the garlic and cook for about a minute.

Add salt, pepper, thyme, and flour and stir for about a minute. Stirring constantly, pour the stock and half and half. Continue stirring until the sauce is thick.

Now the chicken is to be added into the skillet. When the mixture starts boiling, turn down the heat to low heat. Add parsley and frozen peas (do not thaw the peas).

Place biscuits on top. Brush the tops of the biscuits with the beaten egg. Turn off the heat and shift the skillet into the oven.

Set the timer for about 20–25 minutes or until the biscuits are golden brown on top.

Cool for a few minutes before serving.

Garlic Sautéed Cabbage Kale Skillet

Serves: 2

Ingredients:

2 tablespoons unsalted butter

1 small onion, chopped

½ pound kale, lacinato or dinosaur variety, thinly sliced

1 tablespoon chopped fresh parsley

Salt to taste

1 tablespoon oil of your choice

Pepper to taste

¼ head green cabbage, chopped

1 tablespoon vegetable stock or broth

2 cloves garlic, minced

¼ teaspoon red chili flakes

Directions:

Add oil and butter into a skillet and place it over medium-high heat. When butter melts, add onion and cook until pink.

Stir in the cabbage and cook for a few minutes, until it starts browning around the edges.

Stir in the kale, red chili flakes, salt, and pepper. Cook for a couple of minutes or until the kale is slightly tender.

Add stock and scrape the bottom of the pot to remove any browned bits that may be stuck.

Cook for a couple of minutes. Add some more pepper and stir. Garnish with parsley and serve.

Cheesy Cauliflower Soup

Serves: 3

Ingredients:

1 ¾ cups vegetable or chicken broth

½ cup grated extra sharp white cheddar cheese

½ cup grated extra sharp yellow cheddar cheese

⅓ cup cooked, crumbled bacon

½ can (from a 4 ounce can) diced green chilies with its juice

½ onion, chopped

½ large head cauliflower, cut into florets

Salt to taste

½ teaspoon garlic powder

Pepper to taste

¼ cup half and half

½ tablespoon green Tabasco sauce (optional)

Directions:

Pour oil into a heavy skillet and let it heat over medium heat. When the oil is hot, add onion and cook until light brown.

Stir in garlic powder, broth, cauliflower, and salt. Cover and cook until the cauliflower is soft.

Blend with an immersion blender until smooth. Stir in the cheeses and half and half. When cheese melts, stir in the bacon, Tabasco sauce if using, and green chilies. Turn off the heat.

Ladle into soup bowls and serve with croutons or some more cheese if desired.

Taco Soup

Serves: 4

Ingredients:

1 pound ground beef

1 teaspoon minced garlic

½ can (from a 15 ounce can) corn, with its liquid

½ can Rotel tomatoes with green chilies, with its liquid

½ can (from a 15 ounce can) pinto beans, with its liquid

½ can from a (15 ounce can) black beans, with its liquid

1 can (15 ounces) chicken broth

1 small onion, chopped

½ package dry taco seasoning mix

½ package dry ranch dressing mix

4 ounces mild cheddar cheese

Tortilla chips to serve

Directions:

Place a large skillet over medium heat. Add onion, garlic, and beef. Cook until brown. Discard excess cooked fat from the skillet.

Stir in corn, broth, tomatoes, pinto beans, and black beans. When the soup starts boiling, turn down the heat to low heat and simmer for about 15–20 minutes.

Ladle into soup bowls and serve hot, topped with cheese and tortilla chips.

Beef With Penne Pasta

Serves: 2

Ingredients:

½ pound ground beef

1 clove garlic, minced

1 ½ cups uncooked penne pasta

1 ½ cups water

½ teaspoon onion powder

2.5 ounces fresh spinach

1 small onion, chopped

4 ounces tomato sauce

½ cup beef broth

½ can (from a 14 ounce can) diced tomatoes

½ tablespoon Italian seasoning

Salt to taste

Shredded Parmesan cheese to serve (optional)

Directions:

Place a heavy skillet (with a fitting lid) over medium heat.

Add onion and beef and stir. Cook until the meat is not pink anymore. As you stir, break the meat into smaller crumbles.

Stir in garlic. Stir for about a minute.

Stir in broth, tomato sauce, water, tomatoes, Italian seasoning, onion powder, and salt.

Add pasta and stir. When the mixture starts boiling, turn down the heat to low heat and place the lid on the skillet. Cook until pasta is al dente. Stir every now and then.

Scatter spinach on top and continue cooking covered until spinach wilts. Give it a good stir.

Top with Parmesan cheese and serve.

Potato Leek Soup

Serves: 3

Ingredients:

1 ½ tablespoons extra-virgin olive oil, divided

Salt to taste

½ tablespoon white wine vinegar

½ pound Yukon gold potatoes, chopped

1 teaspoon fresh lemon juice

Freshly ground black pepper to taste

Red pepper flakes to taste (optional)

2 cups chopped leeks, white and light green parts only

2 cloves garlic, chopped

2 cups vegetable broth

¾ cup cooked or canned white beans, rinsed, drained

¼ teaspoon Dijon mustard

Pine nuts to garnish

Chopped parsley to garnish

Directions:

Pour 1 tablespoon of oil into a deep skillet and let it heat over medium heat. When the oil is hot, add leeks, pepper, and salt and cook until the leeks are tender.

Stir in garlic and cook for about a minute or until you get a nice aroma.

Add vinegar and stir. Stir in potatoes, broth, and white beans.

When the mixture starts boiling, turn down the heat and cook until the potatoes are soft. Do not cover the pot while cooking.

Turn off the heat and let it cool for a few minutes. Add remaining oil, mustard, and lemon juice. Blend the soup with an immersion blender until smooth. You can also blend the soup in a blender.

Add salt and pepper to taste. Ladle into soup bowls. Garnish with pine nuts, parsley, and red pepper flakes and serve.

Dinner

Skillet Lasagna

Serves: 3

Ingredients:

½ pound ground Italian sausage

½ can (from a 14 ounce can) diced tomatoes

2 cloves garlic, peeled, minced

Salt to taste

6 ounces lasagna noodles, broken

1 can (14 ounces) tomato sauce

1 small onion, diced

¼ teaspoon dried basil

Pepper to taste

½ cup shredded mozzarella cheese

To serve: Optional

Shredded mozzarella cheese

Chopped fresh parsley

Ricotta cheese

Directions:

Place a skillet over medium heat. Add sausage and cook until light brown. As you stir, break the meat into crumbles.

Stir in onion and cook until the meat is brown.

Add garlic and stir for about half a minute. Next stir in the tomatoes and tomato sauce.

Add basil, pepper, and salt and give it a good stir.

Scatter lasagna noodles on top and push the lasagna noodles into the sauce mixture in the skillet.

Keep the pan covered and turn down the heat to medium-low heat. Cook for about 10–15 minutes.

Stir in mozzarella cheese. Turn off the heat. Serve topped with the suggested serving options if desired.

Skillet Beef and Broccoli Ramen

Serves: 5–6

Ingredients:

For the marinade and steak:

½ cup vegetable oil

2 tablespoons red wine vinegar

½ cup low-sodium soy sauce

½ teaspoon salt or to taste

2 teaspoons minced garlic

½ cup honey

½ teaspoon freshly ground black pepper or to taste

⅛ cup chopped Italian flat-leaf parsley

1 ½ pounds sirloin or flank steak, cut into thin slices against the grain

For the noodles:

4 packages (3 ounces each) ramen noodles

6 tablespoons cornstarch

8 cup broccoli florets

2 cups beef broth

4 tablespoons vegetable oil

⅔ cup brown sugar

4 tablespoons sesame oil

4 teaspoons minced garlic

Salt to taste

Pepper to taste

⅔ cup low-sodium soy sauce

½ cup oyster sauce

1 teaspoon grated ginger

To garnish:

Red pepper flakes

Green onion slices

Toasted sesame seeds

Directions:

Add steak slices into a large sealable plastic bag. Combine the rest of the marinade ingredients in a bowl and pour into the bag.

Seal the bag and turn it around a few times so that the steak is well coated with the marinade.

Chill for 1–8 hours depending on how much time you have on hand.

Fill a large skillet with water and bring to a boil over high heat. Add ramen noodles and cook until al dente. Drain in a colander.

Place the skillet back over high heat. When the skillet dries up, add 2 tablespoons of oil into the skillet. When the oil is hot, add half the steak slices and cook undisturbed for a couple of minutes. Flip sides and cook for about a minute. Remove the steak slices onto a plate.

Repeat this process with remaining oil and steak slices.

Combine brown sugar, beef broth, sesame oil, soy sauce, oyster sauce, ginger, and garlic in the skillet and mix well. Keep stirring until the sauce becomes thick.

Let the sauce boil down to about two thirds of its original quantity.

Add broccoli and stir. Cover and cook for a few minutes until the broccoli is crisp as well as tender or cooked to your preference.

Stir in noodles and steak and mix well. Garnish with red pepper flakes, green onion and sesame seeds and serve.

Southwest Ranch Chicken

Serves: 2

Ingredients:

½ pound boneless, skinless chicken breasts, trimmed of fat, halved horizontally

1 ½ tablespoons olive oil

1 small onion, chopped

½ tablespoon minced garlic

½ can diced tomatoes with green chilies

½ can corn

6 tablespoons freshly grated cheddar cheese

½ ounce spicy ranch dressing mix or salad and dressing mix

Chopped cilantro to garnish

2 tablespoons flour

½ tablespoon chicken seasoning

1 red or yellow bell pepper, chopped

½ teaspoon ground cumin

½ can (from a 15 ounce can) black beans, drained

Juice of ½ lime

Directions:

Place the chicken breast slices over a sheet of cling wrap and cover with another wrap. Pound with a meat mallet until they are evenly flattened.

Add flour, salt, and pepper into a shallow bowl. Mix well. Coat the chicken in a flour mixture.

Pour oil into a large skillet and let it heat over medium heat. When the oil is hot, add chicken into the pan and season with half the chicken seasoning. Turn sides after 4 minutes. Sprinkle remaining seasoning on top of the chicken. Once the chicken is well cooked, remove them from the skillet and place on a plate lined with paper towels.

Next add onion into the pan and stir for a few seconds before adding bell pepper, cumin and garlic.

Turn up the heat to medium-high heat and stir often until the vegetables are cooked.

Stir in tomatoes with green chilies, corn, black beans and spicy ranch seasoning mix.

Add the chicken back into the pan and place over the mixture. Sprinkle cheddar cheese on top.

Cook covered on medium heat for a couple of minutes or until the cheese melts.

Garnish with cilantro. Drizzle lime juice on top and serve.

Chicken Noodle Soup

Serves: 4

Ingredients:

1 tablespoon olive oil

½ onion, chopped

2–3 large carrots, sliced

Salt to taste

3 ½ cups chicken broth

2 sprigs thyme or ¼ teaspoon dried thyme

1 bay leaf

3 cloves garlic, peeled, minced

2 small stalks celery, diced

1–1 ¼ pounds bone-in, skinless chicken breasts or thighs

Pepper to taste

1 chicken bouillon cube, crumbled

1 sprig fresh rosemary or ¼ teaspoon dried rosemary

1 cup sort size pasta of your choice

Directions:

Pour oil into a heavy bottomed pan and let it heat over medium heat.

When the oil is hot, add chicken into the pan. Season with salt and pepper.

Cook for about 5 minutes. Turn the chicken over. Season with salt and pepper. Cook for about 5 minutes. Remove the chicken from the skillet and keep it on a plate.

Add onion and celery into the skillet and cook for a couple of minutes. Stir in garlic and cook for another 2 minutes or so. Stir in carrots and some salt to taste.

Cook for about 5 minutes or until the carrots are slightly tender. Keep the chicken over the carrots. Drizzle broth all over the chicken and vegetables. Add rosemary, thyme, and bay leaf. Sprinkle the bouillon cube all over the vegetables and chicken.

When the soup starts boiling, turn down the heat to low heat and cook covered until the chicken is well cooked.

Take out the chicken with a slotted spoon and place it on your cutting board.

Now add the pasta into the skillet. Stir occasionally and cook until the pasta is al dente.

Meanwhile, shred the chicken with a pair of forks and add it back into the skillet only when the pasta is cooked. Do not add the bones.

 Heat thoroughly. Discard the bay leaf, the fresh thyme, and rosemary.

Ladle into soup bowls and serve.

Chicken Gumbo

Serves: 4

Ingredients:

1 pound chicken breasts, boneless, chopped into 1 inch cubes

2 tablespoons oil of your choice

1 clove garlic, minced

1 medium bell pepper, chopped

1 pound fresh okra, cut into ¼ inch thick slices

Salt to taste

2 tomatoes, chopped

1 stalk celery

1 medium onion, chopped

Pepper to taste

1 ½ tablespoons flour

Directions:

Place a heavy skillet over medium heat. Add oil and flour. Stir until the flour. Keep stirring until roux is formed.

Add garlic, onion and bell pepper. Sauté for a few seconds and add about 2 cups of water. Mix well.

Add salt, pepper, tomatoes, okra, chicken, and celery. Bring to a boil.

Turn down the heat to low heat and cook covered for about 15 minutes.

Cover and simmer until the chicken and vegetables are cooked.

Classic Pork Stew

Serves: 4

Ingredients:

1 ¼ pounds pork shoulder, cut into ½ inch chunks

¼ teaspoon salt or to taste

3 slices thick cut bacon, diced

1 tablespoon minced garlic

¼ cup flour

¼ teaspoon pepper or to taste

½ medium onion, diced

2 cups beef stock

1 tablespoon tomato paste

½ teaspoon dried thyme

½ teaspoon dried rosemary

2 medium carrots, cut into 1 inch cubes

1 stalk celery, sliced

2 medium Russet potatoes, cut into 1 inch cubes

½ cup sliced white mushrooms

1 tablespoon Worcestershire sauce

3 tablespoons red wine (optional)

Chopped parsley to garnish

1 bay leaf

Directions:

Place a deep, heavy skillet over medium heat. Add bacon and cook until crisp. When done, remove bacon with a slotted spoon and place on a plate lined with paper towels.

Meanwhile, add salt, flour, and pepper into a shallow bowl and stir. Dredge the pork in the flour mixture. Shake the pork pieces to remove any extra flour.

Place the pork in the skillet and cook until brown all over. Take them out with a slotted spoon and place them on a plate lined with paper towels.

Next add onions into the skillet and cook until translucent.

Stir in garlic and cook for a couple of minutes until you get a nice aroma.

Add Worcestershire sauce, rosemary, broth, tomato paste, red wine if using, and thyme into a bowl and whisk well.

Add a little of this mixture into the skillet. Scrape the bottom of the skillet to remove any browned bits that may be stuck.

Add remaining mixture and stir. Add pork, bacon, carrots, celery, potatoes, mushrooms and bay leaf and mix well.

When the mixture starts boiling, turn down the heat to low heat and cook covered until the meat and vegetables are tender. Stir occasionally.

Serve in bowls. Garnish with parsley and serve.

One Pot Fettuccine Alfredo

Serves: 2

Ingredients:

1 cup milk

4 ounces dried fettuccine

1 clove garlic, minced

Cracked pepper to taste

½ cup chicken stock

1 ½ tablespoons unsalted butter

½ teaspoon salt or to taste

3 tablespoons grated Parmesan cheese + extra to garnish

Directions:

Combine milk, pasta, garlic, seasonings, stock, and butter in a skillet.

Place the skillet over medium-high heat. When the mixture starts boiling, turn down the heat to medium heat and cook until nearly dry and the pasta is cooked.

Turn off the heat. Add Parmesan and stir until the cheese melts.

Garnish with some more pasta and serve.

Desserts

Skillet Berry Cobbler

Serves: 3

Ingredients:

2 cups fresh berries of your choice

¼ cup all-purpose flour

¼ teaspoon salt

½ cup granulated sugar

½ tablespoon cornstarch

For the crumble:

6 tablespoon rolled oats

¼ teaspoon kosher salt

6 tablespoons cold, unsalted butter, cut into small cubes

½ cup all-purpose four

¼ cup sugar

¼ teaspoon ground cinnamon

Directions:

Set the temperature of the oven to 375° F and preheat the oven.

Take a small cast iron skillet or an ovenproof skillet and add berries into it. You can use any one variety of berries or use a mixture of different berries.

Now add sugar, salt, cornstarch, and flour into the skillet and mix well. Spread it evenly.

Combine flour, sugar, cinnamon, salt, and oats in a bowl. Scatter butter over the mixture and mix until crumbly and the mixture comes together when you press some of the mixture.

Scatter the mixture over the berries. Press it lightly. Place the skillet in the oven and set the timer for about 30 minutes or until golden brown on top.

Cool until warm and serve with ice cream if desired.

Skillet Apple Cake

Serves: 4

Ingredients:

<u>For the cake batter:</u>

1 cup all-purpose flour

½ teaspoon baking soda

1 teaspoon baking powder

½ teaspoon ground cinnamon

4 tablespoons butter, melted

1 egg

¼ cup white granulated sugar

½ cup + ⅛ cup buttermilk

1 teaspoon vanilla extract

<u>For the apples:</u>

2 medium apples, peeled, chopped

¼ teaspoon ground cinnamon

¼ cup white granulated sugar

⅛ teaspoon ground nutmeg

Directions:

Set the temperature of the oven to 350° F and preheat the oven. Grease a small cast-iron skillet or an ovenproof skillet with some cooking spray.

To make the cake batter: Add flour, baking soda, baking powder, sugar, and cinnamon into a bowl and mix until well combined.

Measure the butter first and then melt it. Add butter, egg, buttermilk, and vanilla extract and stir until you get smooth batter, making sure not to over mix.

Pour half the batter into the prepared pan. Spread it evenly.

Combine apples, sugar, nutmeg, and cinnamon in a bowl and spread half the apple mixture over the batter in the skillet.

Now pour the remaining batter all over the apples. Scatter remaining apples on top of the batter.

Place the skillet in the oven and set the timer for 30–40 minutes or until the cake is cooked well inside. To check if the cake is done, insert a toothpick in the cake. Remove the toothpick and check if you can see any particles of the cake stuck on it. If so, continue baking for a few more minutes else turn off the oven and take out the skillet.

Cool completely. Cut into wedges and serve.

S'mores Nachos

Serves: 2

Ingredients:

6 Graham crackers

¾ cup semi-sweet chocolate chips

⅓ bag mini marshmallows

Directions:

Set the temperature of the oven to 350° F and preheat the oven. Grease a small cast-iron skillet or an ovenproof skillet with some cooking spray.

Spread graham crackers on the bottom of the skillet. Scatter marshmallows and chocolate chips over the crackers.

Place the skillet in the oven and set the timer for about 15 minutes or until the marshmallows turn golden brown in color. You can broil for a couple of minutes if desired.

Let it cool for about 10 minutes.

Serve.

Crêpes

Serves: 2

Ingredients:

½ cup all-purpose flour

½ tablespoon granulated sugar

¾ cup whole milk

Fresh fruit of your choice to serve

1 large egg

A pinch salt

½ tablespoon butter or more if required

Powdered sugar to garnish

Directions:

Add flour, salt and sugar into a mixing bowl and stir.

Make a big cavity in the center of the flour. Crack the egg into the cavity. Add the milk as well, a little at a time and mix well each timer. Let the batter rest for about 20 minutes.

Place a small skillet over medium heat. Add half the butter. When butter melts, pour half the batter into the skillet and swirl the pan to spread the batter. Turn the crepe over after about 2 minutes. Cook for a few seconds and take out the crepe.

Make the other crepe similarly. Sprinkle powdered sugar over the crepes and serve topped with fresh fruit.

Cheesecakeadilla (Cheesecake Quesadilla)

Serves: 4–8

Ingredients:

1 block cream cheese, softened

½ teaspoon pure vanilla extract

4 tablespoons butter

½ cup sliced strawberries

2 tablespoons powdered sugar

4 flour tortillas

4 teaspoons cinnamon sugar

Melted chocolate to drizzle

Directions:

Add cream cheese, vanilla, and powdered sugar into a bowl and stir until well combined.

Spread two tortillas on a baking sheet. Spread half the cream cheese mixture on each.

Place one tortilla on each, over the cream cheese mixture.

Place a large skillet over medium heat. Add a tablespoon of butter. When butter melts, place a quesadilla in the skillet. When the underside is golden brown, turn the quesadilla over.

Cook the other side until golden brown. Take out the quesadilla from the pan and place on a plate.

Cook the other quesadilla similarly (steps 4–5).

Scatter cinnamon sugar on top. Scatter strawberries on top. Trickle some melted chocolate on top. Cut into wedges and serve.

Chapter 3:

Crockpot and Instant Pot Recipes

Crock Pot Breakfast

Pumpkin Oatmeal

Serves: 6–7

Ingredients:

2 cups steel cut oats

½ cup agave nectar or maple syrup or any other sweetener of your choice to taste

2 small cans pumpkin

4 teaspoons pumpkin pie spice

½ cup butter

4 cups milk

2 teaspoons vanilla

2 tablespoons chia seeds

Directions:

Add oats, sweetener, pumpkin, pumpkin pie spice, butter, milk, vanilla, and chia seeds into a crock pot and stir.

Close the lid and set it on 'Low' with a timer for 8 hours.

Give it a good stir and serve. Store leftover oatmeal in an airtight container after cooling completely and place it in the refrigerator. It can last for 3 to 4 days.

Chile, Cheese, and Scrambled Egg Grits

Serves: 4

Ingredients:

2 ¼ cups chicken broth or vegetable broth

¼ teaspoon ground cumin or more to taste

½ can (from a 4 ounce can) diced green chili peppers with some of the liquid

2 eggs

Salt to taste

½ cup yellow or white grits

6 tablespoons low fat cheddar cheese, shredded

1 clove garlic, peeled, minced

Nonstick cooking spray

Directions:

Place a disposable liner on the bottom of the crock pot. Spray some cooking spray over the liner.

Add broth, cumin, grits, cheese, garlic, salt, and green chili along with a little of the canned liquid into a bowl and stir until well combined.

Pour the mixture into the pot.

Close the lid and set it on 'Low' with a timer for 6–8 hours or on 'High' for 3–4 hours. Stir once after 3 hours. When the timer goes off, switch off the cooker.

Crack eggs into a bowl. Add salt and beat well. Drizzle the eggs over the grits.

Close the pot and let it sit for 30 minutes. Stir well every 15 minutes.

Ladle into bowls and serve.

Greek Eggs Casserole

Serves: 3–4

Ingredients:

6 eggs, beaten

¼ teaspoon salt or to taste

1 small red onion, minced

¼ cup sundried tomatoes

1 cup, chopped spinach

¼ cup milk

½ teaspoon black pepper or to taste

1 clove garlic, minced

½ cup baby Bella mushrooms, sliced

½ teaspoon salt or to taste

⅓ cup crumbled feta cheese

Directions:

Add eggs, milk, salt, and pepper into a bowl. Whisk well. Add onion, garlic, tomatoes, mushrooms and spinach and stir.

Pour the mixture into the crock pot.

Sprinkle cheese on top.

Close the lid and set on 'Low' for 4–5 hours.

Overnight Breakfast Casserole

Serves: 5

Ingredients:

¼ pound bulk breakfast sausage, cooked, crumbled

¼ cup diced yellow onion

½ orange bell pepper, deseeded, diced

½ red bell pepper, deseeded, diced

¼ cup almond milk

½ teaspoon sea salt

Cracked black pepper to taste

1 green onion, thinly sliced

3 ounces bacon, cooked, chopped

½ pound sweet potatoes, peeled, shredded

2 teaspoons ghee, softened, to grease

2 tablespoons full fat coconut milk

8 large eggs, well beaten

½ teaspoon dry mustard

Directions:

Grease the inside of the crock pot with ghee.

Combine sausage, onion, and bacon in a b0wl.

Place the sweet potatoes on the bottom of the crock pot. Spread it all over the bottom of the pot and press it lightly.

Spread the sausage mixture over the sweet potatoes. Scatter the bell peppers over the sausages.

Add eggs, almond milk, coconut milk, salt, pepper and mustard into a bowl and whisk well. Pour the egg mixture all over the sausages and sweet potatoes in the pot.

Close the lid. Set the pot on 'Low' and timer for 6–8 hours.

Lemon Cornmeal Poppy Seed Bread

Serves: 25–28

Ingredients:

For bread:

4 cups all-purpose flour

4 tablespoons poppy seeds

1 teaspoon salt

1 cup butter, melted

1 ½ cups milk

2 tablespoons finely grated lemon zest

1 cup yellow cornmeal

6 teaspoons baking powder

2 cups granulated sugar

6 eggs

4 tablespoons lemon juice

Cooking spray

For glaze:

1 cup powdered sugar

2 tablespoons lemon juice

Directions:

Spray the inside of the crock pot with cooking spray.

To make bread: Add all the dry ingredients into a large bowl, i.e. flour, poppy seeds, salt, cornmeal, and baking powder and mix well.

Add butter, eggs, lemon juice, sugar, and milk into another bowl and mix well. Add mixture of wet ingredients into the bowl of dry ingredients. Mix until well combined.

Pour the batter into the crock pot.

Close the lid. Set on 'High' and timer for 1 ½ to 2 hours or until cooked well inside. To check if it is done, insert a toothpick or knife in the center of the loaf. Remove it and check for any particles that may be stuck on it. If you find any particles, cook for some more time else, switch off the crockpot.

Gently take out the ceramic base from the crockpot and place on a wire rack. Allow it to cool for about 15–20 minutes.

Gently loosen the edges of the loaf with a knife and place on a wire rack. Cool for about an hour.

Meanwhile, make the glaze by stirring together powdered sugar and lemon juice in a bowl. Pour the glaze all over the top of the loaf.

Cut into slices and serve.

Crock Pot Lunch

Chicken Enchilada Soup

Serves: 3

Ingredients:

1 ½ cups enchilada sauce or to taste

½ can (from a 15 ounce can) black beans, drained

1 cup frozen corn

1 ½ pounds chicken thighs, skinless, boneless

Salt to taste

½ teaspoon cayenne pepper

Pepper to taste

3 cups chicken stock

To serve: Optional

Tortilla chips

Sour cream

Chopped cilantro

Grated cheddar cheese

Directions:

Add enchilada sauce, black beans, corn, chicken, salt, cayenne pepper, pepper, and stock into the crock pot. Stir well.

Close the lid and set on 'High' and timer for 2 hours or on 'Low' and timer for 4 hours. Give it a good stir.

Serve in bowls topped with the suggested serving options.

Pumpkin Soup

Serves: 3

Ingredients:

1.3 pounds pumpkin, peeled, deseeded, chopped into chunks

1 small onion, cut into large chunks

1 teaspoon curry powder

Pepper to taste

¼ teaspoon pumpkin pie spice

1 potato, peeled, chopped into chunks

1 ½ teaspoons vegetable bouillon powder mixed with 2 cups hot water or 2 cups hot broth

Salt to taste

½ cup cream

Directions:

Place pumpkin, onion, curry powder, salt, and pepper in the crock pot. Pour water mixed with bouillon or stock into the pot and stir.

Close the lid and set on 'High' for 4–5 hours.

Blend the soup with an immersion blender until smooth. Stir in the cream.

It can be served by itself or with bread.

Greek Lemon and Chicken Soup

Serves: 8

Ingredients:

2.6 pounds chicken breast

4 bay leaves

1 ⅓ cups medium grain white rice, rinsed well

½ cup lemon juice

½ cup flat-leaf parsley

10 cups chicken stock

4 cloves garlic, crushed

4 eggs

5.6 ounces marinated feta in oil, crumbled

½ teaspoon grated lemon zest, to garnish

Salt to taste

5 cups water

Directions:

Add chicken, water, stock, bay leaves, rice and garlic into the crock pot.

Close the lid. Set the pot on 'High' for 4 hours or on 'Low' for 8 hours or until the chicken and rice is cooked.

Take out the chicken from the pot and place in a bowl. Shred the chicken with a pair of forks. Throw away the bay leaves.

Add ¾ of the shredded chicken into the crock pot. Beat eggs and lemon juice in a bowl. Take out about ½ cup of stock from the pot and add into the bowl of eggs, whisking constantly the eggs.

Pour the egg mixture into the crock pot. Set on 'High' and timer for 5–10 minutes or until the soup becomes slightly thick.

Add salt and pepper to taste.

Ladle into soup bowls and serve. Leftover soup should be cooled completely. Transfer the cooled soup into an airtight container in the refrigerator. It can last for 4–5 days.

Chicken Fajita

Serves: 5

Ingredients:

½ can (from a 14.5 ounce can) diced tomatoes with chilies

½ yellow bell pepper, thinly sliced

½ red bell pepper, thinly sliced

½ green bell pepper, thinly sliced

½ orange bell pepper, thinly sliced

3 cloves garlic, minced

1 small onion, thinly sliced

1 ¼ pounds chicken breasts, skinless, boneless

1 teaspoon ground cumin

¼ teaspoon salt or to taste

½ teaspoon smoked paprika

1 teaspoon chili powder

Lime wedges to serve (optional)

¼ teaspoon freshly ground black pepper

Tortillas or lettuce leaves to serve

Directions:

Spray the inside of the crock pot with cooking spray.

Add half the tomatoes into the pot. Spread it evenly. Place half the peppers and half the onions over the tomatoes. Sprinkle garlic all over the peppers.

Place chicken over the peppers.

Mix together cumin, paprika, pepper, and salt in a bowl and sprinkle over the chicken.

Repeat the layers once again with remaining tomatoes over the chicken followed by remaining peppers and onion.

Close the lid. Set on 'Low' for 6—7 hours or on 'High' 3–4 hours.

Serve over tortillas or lettuce leaves with lime wedges if using.

Crock Pot Dinner

American Meatloaf

Makes: 1 meatloaf

Ingredients:

3 pounds ground chuck roast (neck and shoulder cut)

½ cup milk

1 small onion, chopped

¼ cup chopped celery

Ketchup to taste

¼ cup chopped green bell pepper

2 eggs, beaten

3 teaspoons salt or to taste

4 slices bread, crumbled

12 potatoes, cut into cubes

Directions:

Mix together chuck roast, milk, onion, celery, bell pepper, eggs, salt, and bread in a bowl using your hands. Do not over mix else the meat will become tough.

Now shape the dough into a loaf and place it in the crock pot.

Spread ketchup on top of the loaf.

Lay the potato pieces around the sides of the loaf.

Close the lid. Set on 'Low' for 6–7 hours or on 'High 3–4 hours.

Slice and serve warm with potatoes.

Store the leftover meatloaf slices in an airtight container in the refrigerator. Store the potatoes in another airtight container in the refrigerator.

Warm it up and serve. It can last for 4–5 days.

Broccoli Beef

Serves: 2

Ingredients:

¾ pound flank steak, thinly sliced, chopped into 2 inch pieces

⅓ cup low-sodium soy sauce

½ tablespoon sesame oil

⅛ teaspoon red chili flakes or to taste

2–3 cups broccoli florets

½ cup beef broth

¼ cup brown sugar

½ tablespoon garlic, minced

1 tablespoon cornstarch mixed with 2 tablespoons cold water

Salt to taste

Directions:

Spray the crock pot with cooking spray.

Add broth, soy sauce, brown sugar, sesame oil, garlic, and chili flakes into the crock pot. Stir well.

Add steak and stir.

Close the lid. Set on 'Low' for 6–7 hours or on 'High' 3–4 hours.

Add broccoli and cornstarch mixture. Mix well.

Close the lid and cook on 'Low' for 30–40 minutes.

Mix well and serve hot.

Turkey Breast With Gravy

Serves: 3

Ingredients:

1 bone-in turkey breast (2.5–3 pounds), skinless, thawed

1 yellow onion, chopped into chunks

½ cup chicken broth

3 tablespoons butter, divided, chilled, chopped into small cubes

3 stalks celery, chopped

6–8 baby carrots

2 teaspoons arrowroot powder or cornstarch mixed with a tablespoon water

For dry rub:

½ tablespoon dried minced garlic

½ teaspoon paprika

½ teaspoon Italian seasoning

A large pinch dried sage

A large pinch dried parsley

⅛ teaspoon dried thyme

½ teaspoon seasoned salt

¼ teaspoon pepper

Directions:

Grease the crock pot by spraying with cooking spray.

Spread celery on the bottom of the cooker. Scatter half the onion and carrots over the celery. Drizzle chicken broth over it.

To make dry rub: Mix together all the spices in a bowl. Rub this mixture over the turkey. Place the remaining onion and 2 tablespoons butter cubes inside the turkey at different places. Place turkey over the vegetables with the breast side facing down.

The remaining butter is to be melted and brushed over the turkey.

Close the lid. Set on 'Low' for 6–7 hours or on 'High' 3–4 hours or until the internal temperature in the thickest part of the meat shows to 165° F on the meat thermometer.

Remove turkey with a slotted spoon and place on your cutting board. When cool enough to handle, remove the bone, slice and keep warm.

To make gravy: Uncover and cook on 'High' for about 10 minutes. Add arrowroot mixture and stir frequently until thick.

Taste and adjust the seasonings if required.

Serve turkey slices with gravy.

Honey Ginger Chicken

Serves: 6–8

Ingredients:

½ cup chopped onions

2 tablespoons soy sauce

4 tablespoons sherry

3 pounds chicken pieces

3 tablespoons honey

⅓ cup chopped chives

2 tablespoons minced ginger

Directions:

Place the chicken at the bottom of the crock pot. Add onion, soy sauce, sherry, honey, chives, and ginger into a bowl. Mix well and pour over the chicken.

Close the lid. Set on 'Low' for 7–8 hours or on 'High' 4–5 hours.

Mix well and serve. Store leftovers in an airtight container in the refrigerator.

Poached Salmon

Serves: 2–3

Ingredients:

1 cup water

½ lemons, thinly sliced

2 small bay leaves

½ teaspoon black peppercorns

1 pound salmon filets with skin

2 cups dry white wine

2 shallots, thinly sliced

4 sprigs Italian parsley

4 sprigs dill

4 sprigs tarragon

Salt to taste

Freshly ground black pepper to taste

To serve:

Lemon wedges

Coarse sea salt

Extra-virgin olive

Directions:

Add water, lemon slices, bay leaves, dry white wine, shallots, parsley, tarragon, dill, salt, and peppercorns into the crock pot. Stir well.

Sprinkle salt and pepper over the salmon and place in the crock pot with the skin side down.

Close the lid. Set the pot on 'High' and timer for 30 minutes or until the salmon flakes easily when pricked with a fork.

Sprinkle coarse salt on top. Trickle olive oil over the poached salmon and serve with lemon wedges.

Crock Pot Desserts

Pineapple Coconut Tapioca Pudding

Serves: 4–5

Ingredients:

¼ cup small pearl tapioca

1 small egg

¼ cup flaked, sweetened coconut, toasted

6 tablespoons sugar

1 can (13.5 ounces) light coconut milk

¼ cup finely chopped pineapple

Directions:

Grease a crock pot with some cooking spray.

Add tapioca, sugar, and coconut milk into the crock pot and stir.

Close the lid. Set the pot on 'Low' and timer for 60–90 minutes or until most tapioca looks clear and the mixture is more liquid.

Beat egg in a bowl. Whisk in about ¼ cup of the hot liquid from the pot and add it into the pot. Whisk well.

Close the lid and continue cooking for about 20 minutes on 'Low'.

When the timer goes off, add pineapple and stir. Cover the pot and let it rest for an hour.

I suggest you use canned pineapple instead of fresh pineapple because fresh pineapple tends to make it bitter if you do not have the pudding immediately. Leftovers will definitely make it bitter.

Bananas Foster

Serves: 8

Ingredients:

8 bananas, peeled, sliced

2 cups packed brown sugar

2 teaspoons vanilla extract

½ cup chopped walnuts

8 tablespoons butter, melted

½ cup rum

1 teaspoon ground cinnamon

½ cup shredded coconut

Directions:

Place the sliced banana at the bottom of the crock pot.

Measure the butter first and then melt it.

In a bowl, add butter, brown sugar, rum, cinnamon and vanilla extract. Mix well.

Pour over the bananas in the crock pot.

Close the lid. Set the pot on 'Low' and timer for 2 hours.

In the last 30 minutes, sprinkle the walnuts and coconut. Continue cooking for the remaining time.

Serve warm with vanilla ice cream if desired.

Store leftovers in an airtight container in the refrigerator. Warm it up before serving.

Fudge

Serves: 12–15

Ingredients:

7 ounces chocolate chips of your choice

½ teaspoon vanilla extract

½ can (from a 14 ounce can) sweetened condensed milk

½ tablespoon unsalted butter

Directions:

Place chocolate chips, vanilla, condensed milk and butter in a crock pot.

Do not close the lid. Let the pot remain open.

Set the pot to 'Low' and timer for 45 minutes or until the mixture is smooth. Stir every 10–12 minutes.

Meanwhile, grease a small baking dish (about 6 x 6 inches) with some cooking spray.

Line the baking dish with parchment paper as well.

Pour the mixture into the baking dish. Place it in the refrigerator after it cools for 2–6 hours.

Chop into squares and serve.

Cheesecake

Serves: 3

Ingredients:

For the crust:

6 tablespoons Graham cracker crumbs

1 tablespoon granulated sugar

1 tablespoon unsalted butter, melted

For the filling:

¼ cup granulated sugar

½ teaspoon vanilla extract

¼ cup plain yogurt or sour cream

8 ounces cream cheese, at room temperature

1 tablespoon all-purpose flour

1 large egg, at room temperature

Directions:

Grease a small springform pan (about 4 to 5 inches diameter) with some cooking spray.

Place a round parchment (cut to fit onto the bottom) on the bottom of the springform pan.

Pour enough water into the crock pot such that it is about ½ inch in height from the bottom of the pot.

Take three sheets of aluminum foil and crumple each sheet and shape into balls of about 1 inch diameter. Place them in the middle of the crock pot.

Take a large clean kitchen towel and wrap the lid of the crock pot with it.

Make the crust by mixing together Graham cracker crumbs, sugar, and butter in a bowl. Spread the mixture on the bottom as well as a little on the sides of the springform pan. Press the mixture well onto the bottom as well as a little of the sides of the springform pan.

To make filling: Add cream cheese, flour sugar, and vanilla into a blender and blend until well incorporated.

Blend the mixture adding yogurt. Scrape the sides of the bowl whenever required.

Spread the blended mixture over the crust and keep the springform pan in the crock pot over the crumpled foil.

Close the lid along with the wrapped towel. Set the pot on 'High' and timer for about 60–90 minutes or until an instant read thermometer reads 155° F.

Do not uncover for an hour.

Remove the pan from the crock pot and keep it on a wire rack.

Once it cools, place it in the refrigerator for 6–8 hours. Take off the outer ring of the springform pan and peel off the parchment paper. Keep cheesecake on a plate.

Warm up a knife and cut into wedges.

Chocolate Cobbler

Serves: 4

Ingredients:

¼cup butter, melted, divided

½ tablespoon baking powder

½ cup sugar

6 tablespoons milk

¾ cup flour

¼ teaspoon salt

1 ½ tablespoons cocoa powder

For the topping:

6 tablespoons brown sugar

⅛ teaspoon salt

3 tablespoons sugar

¾ tablespoon cocoa powder

Other ingredients:

¾ cup boiling water

Whipped topping or ice cream to serve (optional)

Directions:

Add half the melted butter into the crock pot. Swirl the pot to spread the butter.

Add flour, salt, cocoa, baking powder, and sugar into a mixing bowl and stir until well combined.

Pour remaining melted butter and milk and stir until well incorporated and free from lumps.

Spoon the batter into the crock pot.

To make topping: Add brown sugar, sugar, salt, and cocoa into a bowl and mix well.

Scatter the topping over the batter. You are not to stir the batter after placing the topping. Pour boiling water all over the ingredients.

Close the lid and set on 'Low' for 2–3 hours or for 1 ½ hours on 'High'.

The cobbler will be moist and saucy cake-like.

Cool until warm and serve with suggested serving options.

Poached Pears

Serves: 3

Ingredients:

2 cups red wine

½ teaspoon vanilla extract

1 whole star anise

¼ cup sugar

1 stick cinnamon (about 2 inches)

3 firm pears, peeled, cored

Directions:

Add vanilla extract, red wine, and sugar into the crock pot and stir.

Stir in star anise and cinnamon sticks. Drop the pears into the crock pot and turn it around in the mixture.

Close the lid and set the pot on 'Low' and timer for 3–4 hours or until the pears are cooked.

To serve: Take out the pears from the crock pot and place in serving bowls. If the sauce is very thin, pour it into a saucepan and cook on the stovetop until thick, like syrup.

Drizzle the sauce over the pears.

Serve.

PS: A scoop or two of vanilla ice cream goes perfectly with them.

Peanut Clusters

Serves: 10–12

Ingredients:

½ pound white chocolate melting bar

½ cup semi-sweet chocolate chips

2 ounces German chocolate baking bar

8 ounces dry roasted peanuts

Directions:

Add German chocolate, white chocolate, and chocolate chips into the crock pot.

Scatter peanuts on top of the chocolate.

Close the lid and set the cooker on 'High' and timer for 45 minutes. You are not to uncover or stir the mixture until the time is up.

Now give it a good stir and set the pot on 'High' once again and timer for 45 minutes. Now stir the mixture at 15 minute intervals.

Line a baking sheet with parchment paper. Drop tablespoonful (or any size as preferred) of the mixture on the baking sheet, leaving some gap between the clusters. Make sure every cluster has peanuts in it.

Let it cool completely. Peel off the parchment paper. Transfer into an airtight container until use.

Apple Pudding Cake

Serves: 15–18

Ingredients:

4 cups all-purpose flour

6 teaspoons baking powder

1 cup cold butter

8 apples, peeled, cored, diced

1 cup honey or light brown sugar

2 teaspoons ground cinnamon

1 ⅓ cups + ½ cup sugar, divided

½ teaspoon salt or more to taste

2 cups milk

3 cups orange juice

¼ cup butter, melted

Directions:

Add 1 ⅓ cups sugar, flour, salt, and baking powder into a bowl and stir until well combined.

Add cold butter into the mixture and cut it into the flour mixture until the mixture is coarse and crumbly.

Add milk and stir until just combined.

Spray some cooking spray on the bottom as well as sides of the crock pot.

Pour the batter into the crock pot.

Scatter apples all over the top of the batter.

Add orange juice, melted butter, cinnamon, ½ cup sugar, and honey into a bowl and mix well.

Pour this mixture all over the apples.

Take a large clean kitchen towel and wrap the lid of the crock pot with it.

Close the lid along with the wrapped towel. Set the pot on 'High' and timer for about 3–4 hours.

Do not uncover for an hour.

Slice once it is warm and serve.

Instant Pot Breakfast

Peaches and Cream Steel Cut Oats

Serves: 2

Ingredients:

1 cup steel cut oats

½ peach pitted, chopped

½ teaspoon vanilla extract

2 cups water

To serve: Optional

Maple syrup

Chopped almonds

1 tablespoon flaxseed meal

Milk, as required

Directions:

Add oats, peach, vanilla, and water into the instant pot and mix well.

Close and lock the lid. Set the pot on 'Manual' option and timer for 3 minutes. When the timer goes off, let the pressure release naturally for 10 minutes, after which it quickly releases excess pressure.

Serve warm with suggested serving options if using.

Cranberry Orange French Toast

Serves: 10–12

Ingredients:

For cranberry orange sauce:

4 cups fresh cranberries

1 cup granulated sugar

½ teaspoon salt

½ teaspoon ground cinnamon

½ cup orange juice

For French toast:

½ cup butter, melted

4 cups milk

2 tablespoons orange zest, grated or to taste

1 cup sugar

6 eggs, beaten

½ teaspoon salt

2 teaspoons vanilla

½ loaf challah bread or French bread, cubed

Directions:

To make sauce: Add cranberries, sugar, salt, cinnamon, and orange juice into the instant pot. Stir.

Set the pot on 'Sauté' option and cook until cranberries burst and the sauce is slightly thick. Press the 'Cancel' button.

Pour the sauce into a greased, heat proof pan that fits in the instant pot.

Clean the pot and pour about 1 ½ cups of water into the instant pot and keep a trivet in the pot.

Meanwhile mix together butter and sugar in a bowl. When sugar dissolves, mix in the orange zest, eggs, salt, and vanilla set aside for 5 minutes or until the bread absorbs all the liquid.

Spread the bread mixture over the sauce in the pan. Place the pan inside the instant pot, over the trivet with the help of foil sling.

Close and lock the lid. Set pot on 'Manual' option and timer for 20 minutes. When the timer goes off let the pressure release naturally for 10 minutes after which it quickly releases excess pressure.

Cool and serve warm or at room temperature.

Omelet Casserole

Serves: 2–3

Ingredients:

5 tablespoons grated mozzarella cheese

¼ green bell pepper, diced

3 eggs

Chopped parsley, to garnish

½ cup diced mushrooms

½ cup roasted potatoes or leftover cooked potatoes

2 tablespoons milk or cream (optional)

Directions:

Take a small ramekin or casserole dish and grease with oil. Scatter about 2 tablespoons of mozzarella cheese on the bottom of the dish.

Combine potatoes, bell pepper, and mushrooms in a bowl.

Scatter the vegetables over the cheese in the dish.

Crack the eggs into a bowl and whisk well. Add milk and whisk well. Add 2 tablespoons of cheese and whisk well.

Pour the egg mixture all over the vegetables.

Pour about 1 ½ cups of water into the instant pot. Place a trivet or rack in the pot. Place the dish over the rack.

Close and lock the lid. Set the pot on 'Manual' option and timer for 10 minutes. When the timer goes off, let the pressure release naturally.

Garnish with remaining cheese and parsley and serve. You can garnish with extra cheese if desired.

Hash Brown Breakfast Casserole

Serves: 3

Ingredients:

3 strips bacon, diced

⅔ cup shredded cheddar cheese, divided + extra to tarnish

⅛ cup light cream

2 small green onions, sliced

Freshly ground pepper to taste

¾ cup frozen hash brown potatoes, defrosted

4 large eggs

¼ cup diced red bell pepper

Salt to taste

Chopped parsley or parsley to garnish

Directions:

Grease a small springform pan with some cooking spray or butter.

Press the 'Sauté' button and add bacon and cook until crisp. Take out the bacon from the pot and place over layers of paper towels. Press the 'Cancel' button and drain off all the cooked fat from the pot.

Wipe the pot with paper towels. Pour 2 cups of water into the instant pot. Place a trivet or rack in the pot.

Spread hash browns on the bottom of the springform pan. Sprinkle ½ cup cheese over the hash browns.

Crack eggs into a bowl. Add cream and whisk well. Add bell pepper, pepper, salt, bacon and green onion and stir. Drizzle the mixture all over the cheese in the springform pan.

Scatter remaining cheese on top. Make a sling with foil and place the springform pan on the trivet.

Close and lock the lid. Set the pot on 'Manual' and timer for 30 minutes. Let the pressure release naturally.

Lift the pan out of the instant pot with the help of the sling. Let it cool for about 15 minutes.

Slice and serve with parsley and some more cheese.

Christmas Morning Breakfast Casserole

Serves: 8

Ingredients:

12 large eggs

Pepper to taste

1 teaspoon dried thyme

1 teaspoon garlic powder

8 frozen, fully cooked sausage patties

8 slices bacon, cooked until crisp, chopped into large pieces

½ teaspoon salt or to taste

½ cup milk

1 teaspoon onion powder

1 pound frozen tater tots

1 cup grated cheddar cheese

Directions:

Crack eggs into a bowl and beat well. Add salt, pepper, thyme, garlic powder, milk, and onion powder and whisk well.

Spread tater tots on the bottom of a heat proof pan and fit well inside the instant pot.

Lay the sausage patties over the tater tots. Drizzle the egg mixture all over the patties and tater tots. Scatter cheese on top followed by bacon.

Keep the dish covered with foil. Make a sling with aluminum foil for the pan so that it can be easily picked or kept inside the instant pot.

Pour 1 ½ cups of water into the instant pot. Place a rack or trivet in the pot. Lift the pan with the help of the sling and keep it on the trivet.

Close and lock the lid. Set the pot on 'Manual' and timer for 30 minutes. Let the pressure release naturally.

Lift the pan out of the instant pot with the help of the sling. Let it cool for about 15 minutes.

Slice and serve.

Instant Pot Lunch

Hearty Chicken Minestrone

Serves: 3

Ingredients:

6 cups chicken broth or water

¾ pound chicken, skinless, boneless

½ can (from a 15 ounce can) diced tomatoes

½ can (from a 15 ounce can) chickpeas, drained, rinsed

2 cups Swiss chard

1 small zucchini, chopped

2 cups cabbage, shredded

½ cup whole-wheat pasta

Salt to taste

Pepper to taste

Directions:

Add broth, chicken, tomatoes, chickpeas, Swiss chard, zucchini, cabbage, and pasta into the instant pot.

Close and lock the lid. Set the pot on the 'Soup' option.

When the timer goes off, let the pressure release naturally for about 5 minutes and then remove excess pressure.

Add salt and pepper to taste.

Serve hot.

Beef and Macaroni Soup

Serves: 4

Ingredients:

½ pound extra lean ground beef

1 clove garlic, minced

½ tablespoon Worcestershire sauce (optional but recommended)

½ jar (from a 26 ounce jar) tomato pasta sauce

½ cup frozen spinach

½ red bell pepper, chopped

¾ cup whole-grain elbow macaroni, uncooked

1 medium onion, chopped

1 cup low-sodium beef broth

Salt to taste

Pepper to taste

1 can (14 ounces) diced tomatoes

Directions:

Set the pot on 'Sauté' option. Press the 'Adjust' button once. Add beef and onion and cook until beef turns brown. As you stir, break the meat into smaller pieces.

Add garlic and sauté for about a minute or until you get a nice aroma. Press the 'Cancel' button.

Add Worcestershire sauce, tomato pasta sauce, spinach, bell pepper, macaroni, diced tomatoes, broth, salt, and pepper into the instant pot.

Close the lid. Set the pot on the 'Soup' option.

When the timer goes off, let the pressure release naturally for 5 minutes. Now remove excess pressure. Stir well and serve.

Creamy Chicken and Mushroom Soup

Serves: 8

Ingredients:

2 onions, thinly sliced

4 cups chopped mushrooms

2 pounds chicken breasts, skinless, boneless, chopped into chunks

Salt to taste

2 teaspoons Italian seasoning or poultry seasoning

6 cloves garlic, peeled, minced

2 yellow squash, peeled, deseeded, chopped

5 cups chicken stock

Pepper to taste

Directions:

Add onions, mushrooms, chicken, salt, seasonings, garlic, squash, and stock into the instant pot and stir.

Close and lock the lid. Set the pot on the 'Poultry' option.

When the timer goes off, let the pressure release naturally for 5 minutes, after which it quickly releases excess pressure.

Quinoa Burrito Bowls

Serves: 2

Ingredients:

½ teaspoon extra-virgin olive oil

½ bell pepper, diced

½ teaspoon ground cumin

½ cup prepared salsa

1 small red onion, diced

Salt to taste

½ cup quinoa, rinsed

½ cup water

¾ cup cooked or canned black beans

To serve: Optional

2 lettuce leaves, shredded

Chopped avocado

Guacamole

Salsa

Cilantro

Any other toppings of your choice

Directions:

Set the pot on 'Sauté' option. Add oil to the instant pot and allow it to heat. When the oil is hot, add onion and bell pepper and cook until slightly tender.

Stir in the cumin and salt. Stir for a few seconds until aromatic.

Add quinoa, salsa, beans, and water and stir.

Close the lid. Select 'Rice' option. When the timer goes off, fluff the quinoa grains with a fork.

Divide quinoa into two bowls. Serve with any of the suggested serving options.

Vegetable Rice

Serves: 4–5

Ingredients:

2 cups rice of your choice (short, medium, or long grain), rinsed, soaked in water for 30 minutes, drained

2 teaspoons minced garlic

4 tablespoons oil of your choice

1 cup frozen peas

3 cups vegetable stock

2 teaspoons salt or to taste

1 cup chopped onion

2 teaspoons grated ginger

1 cup diced carrots

1 cup sliced green beans

1 cup chopped parsley or cilantro

2 teaspoons pepper or to taste

4 bay leaves

2 sticks cinnamon (1 inch each)

Directions:

Pour oil into the instant pot. Set the pot on 'Sauté' option. Let the oil heat.

When the oil is hot, add onion and cook for a couple of minutes.

Stir in bay leaves, cinnamon, ginger, and garlic. Cook for about a minute or until you get a nice aroma.

Stir in carrots, green beans, and peas. Stir for about a minute.

Now add rice and mix well. Stir for a couple of minutes or until rice is well coated with the oil.

Stir in stock, cilantro, pepper, and salt.

Close and lock the lid. Select 'Rice' option.

When the timer goes off, let the rice rest for about 15 minutes.

Fluff the rice grains with a fork and serve.

Warm Bean Salad

Serves: 6

Ingredients:

½ can (from a 15.5 ounce can) cannellini beans, rinsed, drained

½ can (from a 15.5 ounce can) kidney beans, rinsed, drained

½ can (from a 15.5 ounce can) corn, rinsed, drained

2 ripe tomatoes, chopped

½ pound green beans, stringed, cut into 1 inch pieces

2 tablespoons vinegar or to taste

½ teaspoon pickling spice

⅓ cup water

¼ teaspoon mustard seeds

½ teaspoon hot pepper sauce to taste

Directions:

Add cannellini beans, kidney beans, corn, beans, vinegar, pickling spice, water, mustard seeds, and hot sauce into the instant pot and stir.

Close and lock the lid. Set the pot on the 'Manual' option and set the timer for 5 minutes.

When the timer goes off, let the pressure release naturally for 5 minutes, after which it quickly releases excess pressure.

Uncover, stir and transfer into a bowl. Add tomatoes and mix well.

Serve warm.

Red Beans and Rice

Serves: 3

Ingredients:

2 teaspoons olive oil

½ onion, chopped

7 ounces smoked turkey sausage, sliced

½ can (from a 15 ounce can) kidney beans, rinsed, drained

3 tablespoons tomato paste

1 teaspoon Cajun seasoning or to taste

Hot sauce to taste (optional)

1 celery stalk, sliced

½ green bell pepper, diced

2 cups chicken broth

1 cup long grain white rice, rinsed, soaked in water for 20 minutes

2 small bay leaves

⅛ teaspoon cayenne pepper or to taste

Salt to taste

Directions:

Pour oil into the instant pot. Select the 'Sauté' button and press the 'Adjust' button once. When the oil is hot, add onion, celery, and green bell pepper and cook for a couple of minutes.

Stir in sausage. Cook until the sausage is brown. Add rice and mix well. Stir often for about 2 minutes.

Stir in beans, broth, tomato paste, Cajun seasoning, bay leaves, cayenne pepper, and salt and stir.

Close and lock the lid. Press 'Rice' option. When done, fluff the rice with a fork.

Serve topped with hot sauce if desired.

One Pot Spaghetti

Serves: 3

Ingredients:

½ pound lean ground beef

3 cloves garlic, minced

½ can (from a 15 ounce can) diced tomatoes

½ tablespoon Italian seasoning

½ teaspoon pepper or to taste

6 ounces dried spaghetti noodles, broken into half

Chopped parsley to garnish

½ onion, diced

½ can (from a 15 ounce can) tomato sauce

1 ½ cups water

Salt to taste

½ teaspoon sugar

⅓ cup shredded Parmesan cheese or more to taste

Directions:

Select the 'Sauté' button. Press the 'Adjust' button once. Add beef and onion and stir. Cook until brown. As you stir, break the meat into smaller pieces. Discard any excess cooked fat from the pot.

Stir in garlic and cook for about a minute or until you get a nice aroma.

Add tomato sauce, water, and tomatoes with its liquid.

Stir in salt, Italian seasoning, sugar, and pepper.

Add spaghetti and press it lightly so that they are immersed in the liquid in the pot.

Press the 'Cancel' button.

Close and lock the lid. Select 'Manual' and set the timer for 5 minutes.

When the timer goes off, quick release excess pressure.

Add Parmesan and parsley and mix well.

Serve hot.

Instant Pot Dinner

Vegetable and Tofu Curry

Serves: 8

Ingredients:

2 pounds extra-firm tofu

2 cups vegetable broth

2 tablespoons minced fresh ginger

Salt to taste

2 medium onions, chopped

1 ½ cups frozen peas

2 small eggplants, chopped

3 cups sliced, assorted bell peppers

6–8 tablespoons Thai green or red curry paste

2 cans (14.5 ounces each) coconut milk

2 tablespoons coconut sugar or regular sugar

1 teaspoon turmeric powder

1 tablespoon oil

To serve: Optional

Hot cooked brown rice

Hot cooked quinoa

Directions:

You need to press the tofu of excess moisture. For this, take out the tofu from the package and place it on a plate lined with paper towels. Place something heavy over the tofu like a cold drink can or heavy pan. Let it remain this way for at least 30 minutes. If you can keep it for 1 to 2 hours, that would be great.

Select 'Sauté' option. Press the 'Adjust' button once. Add oil and wait for it to heat. When the oil is hot, add tofu and cook until golden brown all over. Do not crowd the pot, you can add in batches and cook them.

Remove the tofu with a slotted spoon onto a plate and set aside.

Add more oil if required. Add onion and cook until translucent. Add turmeric and ginger and stir for a few seconds until you get a nice aroma. Press the 'Cancel' button.

Add ginger, salt, peas, eggplants, bell peppers, tofu, curry paste, coconut milk, and sugar and mix well.

Close and lock the lid. Select the 'Manual' option and set the timer for 7 minutes. When the timer goes off, quick release excess pressure.

If there is too much liquid in the pot, press the 'Sauté' button, simmer for a few minutes until the desired thickness is achieved.

Stir and serve over cooked quinoa or brown rice.

Dump Bean Soup

Serves: 4

Ingredients:

½ can (from a 15 ounce can) black beans

½ can (from a 15 ounce can) cannellini beans

½ can (from a 15 ounce can) refried beans

½ can (from a 15 ounce can) kidney beans

½ can (from a 15 ounce can) butter beans

½ can (from a 14 ounce can) chopped tomatoes with its liquid

½ teaspoon minced garlic

Pepper to taste

1 ½ cups water

½ teaspoon onion powder

Directions:

Add refried beans into the instant pot. Add water and mix well. Add all the beans, tomatoes, garlic, pepper, and onion powder and mix well.

Close and lock the lid. Select the 'Manual' option. Set the timer for 10 minutes.

When the timer goes off, let the pressure release naturally for 10 minutes after which, it quickly releases excess pressure.

Stir and serve.

Turkey Noodle Soup

Serves: 8

Ingredients:

4 cups chopped turkey

8 cups chicken stock

1 large onion, chopped

½ cup celery, chopped

1 carrot, chopped

2 cloves garlic, minced

1 small packet egg noodles

Salt to taste

1 bay leaf

2 tablespoons parsley, chopped

Pepper to taste

Directions:

Spray the cooking pot of the instant pot with some cooking spray. Add onion, garlic, celery, and carrots and cook for a couple of minutes.

Stir in turkey and cook for about 3 to 4 minutes. Stir in the stock.

Close and lock the lid. Select the 'Poultry' button and the timer for 15 minutes.

Quick release excess pressure. Add egg noodles and stir.

Close and lock the lid. Set the pot on 'Poultry' and timer for 5 minutes.

When the timer goes off, let the pressure release naturally for 10 minutes, after which it quickly releases excess pressure.

Stir and serve garnished with parsley.

BBQ Turkey

Serves: 4–5

Ingredients:

¾ cup chicken broth

1 tablespoon apple cider vinegar

1 tablespoon Worcestershire sauce

½ tablespoon soy sauce

1 small onion, thinly sliced

½ cup ketchup (without sugar)

2 packets stevia

½ tablespoon mustard

1 ½ pounds turkey breast, skinless, boneless

1 clove garlic, minced

Directions:

Add chicken broth, vinegar, Worcestershire sauce, soy sauce, ketchup, stevia, mustard, and garlic into a bowl and whisk well.

Spray the cooking pot of the instant pot with cooking spray. Place onions in the pot and cook until translucent. Sprinkle salt and pepper over the turkey and place in the pot. Mix well. Cook for a couple of minutes. Add sauce mixture and mix well.

Close and lock the lid. Select 'Poultry' option. When the timer goes off, let the pressure release naturally.

Remove turkey with a slotted spoon and place on your cutting board. When cool enough to handle, shred the turkey. You can also slice the turkey if desired.

Check for the liquid in the pot. If there is too much liquid, you can add a teaspoon of cornstarch mixture mixed with water and cook on 'Sauté' option until the thickness you desire is achieved. Stir constantly.

Add turkey and mix well. Heat well.

Serve immediately.

Cherry Tomato Chicken Cacciatore

Serves: 2—3

Ingredients:

½ teaspoon olive oil

½ pound cherry tomatoes, crushed lightly

¼ teaspoon red pepper flakes

½ teaspoon dried oregano

⅛ cup tart red table wine

1 ½ pounds bone in chicken legs and thighs

1 clove garlic, crushed

Salt or to taste

4 fresh basil, torn

½ cup water

¼ cup green olives, pitted

Directions:

Press the 'Sauté' button. Press the 'Adjust' button once. Add oil and wait for the oil to heat. Add chicken and cook until brown all over. Remove the chicken from the pot and set it aside on a plate.

Add garlic and sauté for a few seconds until fragrant. Add salt, oregano, red pepper flakes, tomatoes, wine, and water. Scrape the bottom of the pot to remove any browned bits.

Add the chicken back into the pot and stir well. Press the 'Cancel' button.

Close and lock the lid. Select 'Poultry' option. When the timer goes off, quick release excess pressure.

Garnish with olives and basil and serve.

Chinese Vegetable Rice

Serves: 4

Ingredients:

2 cups short grain rice or any other rice of your choice, rinsed well, soaked in water for 30 minutes

1–2 tablespoons dark soy sauce or to taste (optional)

1–2 tablespoons soy sauce or to taste

2 tablespoons oyster sauce

2 cups water

2–4 teaspoons sugar (optional)

2 tablespoons sesame oil

4 cloves garlic, minced

1 medium carrot, diced

2 heads Bok Choy, chopped

1 cup diced ham (optional)

2 scallions, sliced

8 mushrooms, sliced

¼ cup edamame

Any other vegetables of your choice

Hot sauce to taste (optional)

Sesame seeds to garnish (optional)

Directions:

Combine rice, sugar, soy sauce, dark soy sauce if using, oyster sauce, sugar, sesame oil and water in the instant pot.

Scatter garlic, carrot, Bok Choy, ham, scallions, mushrooms, edamame, and any other vegetables if using, over the rice. Do not stir.

Close and lock the lid. Select 'Rice' option. Stir and serve garnished with sesame seeds and hot sauce.

One Pot Spicy Sausage Pasta

Serves: 3

Ingredients:

½ tablespoon olive oil

½ pound spicy Italian sausage

½ tablespoon Italian seasoning

1 can (28 ounces) crushed tomatoes

6 tablespoons pesto

1 ½ – 2 cups shredded kale

Salt to taste

½ medium onion, diced

½ tablespoon minced garlic

¼ teaspoon red pepper flakes

1 ½ cups water

½ pound rigatoni pasta

1 cup shredded mozzarella cheese

Chopped parsley to garnish

Pepper to taste

Directions:

Select the 'Sauté' button. Press the 'Adjust' button once. Add oil and let it heat. When the oil is hot, add sausage and cook until brown. As you stir, crumble the meat.

Stir in red pepper flakes, Italian seasoning and garlic and cook for about a minute or until you get a nice aroma. Make sure you do not burn the spices. Press the 'Cancel' button.

Stir in tomatoes, kale, pasta, water, and 4 tablespoons pesto. Season with salt and pepper.

Close and lock the lid. Select 'Manual' and set the timer for 5 minutes.

When the timer goes off, quick release excess pressure.

Add remaining pesto and stir. Sprinkle cheese on top. Close the lid and let it sit for a few minutes until the cheese melts.

Garnish with parsley and serve.

Instant Pot Desserts

Raspberry Curd

Serves: 4

Ingredients:

6 ounces fresh raspberries

1 tablespoon fresh lemon juice

1 tablespoon butter

½ cup sugar

1 egg yolk

Directions:

Combine sugar, raspberries, and lemon juice in the instant pot.

Close and lock the lid. Select 'Manual' and timer for 1 minute. When the timer goes off, let the pressure release naturally for 5 minutes and then release excess pressure.

Strain the raspberries through a fine wire mesh strainer or a food mill and discard the seeds.

Add yolk into a bowl and whisk well. Whisking constantly, pour the hot raspberry mixture into the bowl of yolk. Pour it into the instant pot and stir.

Press 'Sauté' option and let the mixture start boiling. Stir continuously for a couple of minutes. Press 'Cancel' and add butter. Stir until butter melts.

Pour into an airtight container. Let it cool completely. Chill until use.

Apple Crisp

Serves: 8

Ingredients:

<u>For the topping:</u>

1 cup all-purpose flour

1 cup light brown sugar

¼ teaspoon salt

1 cup old-fashioned rolled oats

1 teaspoon ground cinnamon

¾ cup unsalted butter, cut into small cubes

<u>For the filling:</u>

8 small Granny Smith apples, cored, peel if desired, cut into 1 inch chunks

2 tablespoons lemon juice

½ cup light brown sugar

¼ teaspoon salt

4 tablespoons butter, melted

1 teaspoon vanilla extract

1 teaspoon ground cinnamon

1 ½ cups water

Directions:

Spray the inside of the instant pot with cooking spray.

To make filling: Add lemon juice, brown sugar, salt, butter, vanilla, and cinnamon into the instant pot and stir.

Add apples and stir.

To make the topping: Combine flour, sugar, salt, oats, and cinnamon in a bowl.

Add butter cubes and mix until crumbly.

Scatter the topping mixture on top of the apple mixture in the pot.

Close and lock the lid. Select the 'Manual' option and set the timer for 1 minute. When the timer goes off, quick release excess pressure.

If you want a crisp top, spoon the apple crisp in oven safe bowls. Broil for a couple of minutes, until the top is golden brown.

Chocolate Peanut Butter Cheesecake

Serves: 4–5

Ingredients:

7–8 crème filled chocolate sandwich cookies, finely crushed, divided

10 ounces Philadelphia cream cheese, softened, divided

¼ teaspoon vanilla extract

1 egg

½ cup thawed whipped topping

1 tablespoon butter, melted

2 ounces baker's semi-sweet chocolate, melted

5 ½ tablespoons sugar, divided

⅛ cup creamy peanut butter

Directions:

Add ½ cup cookie crumbs into a bowl. Add butter and mix until crumbly.

Grease a small springform pan with cooking spray. Keep the bottom of the pan wrapped with foil.

Add the cookie crumb mixture into the pan and press it well onto the bottom of the pan.

Place about 7 ounces of cream cheese in a bowl. Beat with an electric hand mixer until it is creamy.

Beat in the vanilla, melted chocolate and 4 tablespoons of sugar.

Beat in the egg at low speed. Spoon the mixture over the crust and spread it evenly.

Pour 2 cups of water into the instant pot. Place a trivet inside the pot.

Place the pan on the trivet with the help of an aluminum sling.

Cover the lid and lock it. Set the pot on 'Manual' and timer for 40 minutes. Let the pressure release naturally. The middle of the cheesecake will be slightly jiggling a bit and that is perfectly ok.

Take out the pan with the help of the sling and keep it on a wire rack. Discard the foil wrapper.

Loosen the edges of the cheesecake by running a knife around the edges. Remove the sides of the springform pan and allow it to come to room temperature.

Place the cheesecake in the refrigerator for at least 4 hours.

Meanwhile, combine remaining sugar and remaining cream cheese in a bowl. Beat with an electric hand mixer until creamy. Beat in the peanut butter.

Beat in cool whip until just incorporated, making sure not to over beat.

Spoon the topping over the cheesecake. Scatter remaining cookie crumbs on top.

Chill until use. Cut into wedges and serve.

Blueberry Bread Pudding

Serves: 3

Ingredients:

½ cup half and half

5 tablespoons sugar, divided

2 cups cubed croissants

2 ounces cream cheese, cut into small pieces

2 eggs

½ teaspoon grated lemon zest

½ cup blueberries

Directions:

Beat eggs in a bowl. Add half and half, lemon zest, and 3 tablespoons sugar and beat until well incorporated.

Stir in cream cheese, blueberries, and croissants. Let it soak for 10 minutes.

Prepare a heat proof pan that can fit inside the instant pot by greasing it with oil or butter.

Spread the bread mixture in the pan and press it lightly. Keep the dish covered with foil.

Pour about 1 ½ cups of water into the instant pot. Place a trivet in the pot. Using slings made of aluminum foil, place the pan on the trivet.

Close and lock the lid. Select 'Manual' and set the timer for 25 minutes. When the timer goes off, let the pressure release naturally.

Take a knife and pierce it in the custard. Remove the knife and check if there are any particles stuck on it. If so, close and lock the lid and cook on 'Manual' option for 5 minutes. Let the pressure release naturally for 5 to 6 minutes after which, quickly release excess pressure.

Take out the pan. Scatter remaining sugar on top and broil in a preheated oven until sugar is caramelized or you can use a culinary torch to caramelize the top.

Strawberries 'n' Cream Rice Pudding

Serves: 8

Ingredients:

1 cup short grain rice, rinsed well, soaked in water for 1 hour, drained

2 cups diced fresh strawberries

2 tablespoons strawberry jam

½ teaspoon ground nutmeg

Cinnamon sticks to garnish

4 cups milk

4 tablespoons sweetened condensed milk

1 teaspoon ground cinnamon

8 whole strawberries

Directions:

Add rice, milk, nutmeg, ground cinnamon and condensed milk into the instant pot and stir.

Close the lid and lock it. Select 'Manual' and set on 'Low pressure' option. Set the timer for 8 minutes.

When the timer goes off, release excess pressure. Uncover and add strawberries and strawberry jam.

Mix well. Close the lid once again. Set the timer for 2 minutes. Let the pressure release naturally for 10 minutes after which, quickly release excess pressure.

Pour into a bowl. Let it cool completely. Chill until use.

Serve in bowls garnished with a cinnamon stick and a strawberry.

Chocolate Cake

Serves: 14–16

Ingredients:

1 ½ cups all-purpose flour

1 cup sugar

1 teaspoon baking soda

1 ½ teaspoons baking powder

1 ½ cups cocoa powder

½ teaspoon salt

1 cup milk

2 teaspoons vanilla extract

1 cup melted butter

6 eggs

Directions:

Sift together flour, baking powder, baking soda, and cocoa into a mixing bowl. Sprinkle sugar and salt and mix well.

Beat eggs in a bowl along with melted butter, milk, and vanilla. Pour the egg mixture into the mixing bowl with dry ingredients and stir until well combined and smooth.

Prepare a cake pan by placing butter paper or parchment paper on the bottom of the pan.

Spoon the batter into the pan. Keep the pan covered with aluminum foil.

Add about 2 cups of water into the instant pot. Keep a trivet or rack in the pot.

Using slings made of aluminum foil, place the pan inside the pot, on the trivet.

Close and lock the lid. Select 'Manual' and timer for 40 minutes.

When the timer goes off, let the pressure release naturally.

Take out the cake pan with the help of the slings and let it cool until warm. Top with icing sugar.

Cut into slices and serve. Store leftover cake in an airtight container in the refrigerator. It can last for about 15 days.

Chapter 4:

Baking Recipes

Breakfast

French Toast Bake

Serves: 8

Ingredients:

16 thick bread slices, torn

6 eggs

4 tablespoons ground cinnamon

½ teaspoon salt

2 cups milk

½ cup sugar

2 tablespoons vanilla extract

1 ½ cups blueberries

To serve:

Maple syrup

Butter

Directions:

Line the bottom of a baking dish with a round piece of parchment paper.

Scatter the bread pieces over the parchment paper.

Crack the eggs into a bowl and whisk well. Add cinnamon, salt, vanilla, and sugar and whisk until well combined.

Add milk and stir until well combined. Pour the egg mixture all over the bread pieces. Stir lightly but make sure that the bread is well coated with the mixture.

Scatter blueberries on top and stir lightly.

Set the temperature of the oven to 350° F and preheat the oven.

Place the baking dish in the oven. Set the timer for about 30 minutes or until cooked through. Insert a knife in the center of the French toast and take it out. Check for any sticky particles on the knife. If you find any, bake for some more time.

Serve with the suggested serving options if desired or serve with some other toppings of your choice.

German Pancakes

Serves: 3

Ingredients:

3 tablespoons butter, chopped into ½ inch cubes

½ cup flour

½ tablespoon sugar

⅛ teaspoon salt

½ cup milk of your choice

3 large eggs

½ teaspoon vanilla extract

To serve: Optional

Powdered sugar

Syrup

Fresh fruit

Any other toppings of your choice

Directions:

Set the temperature of the oven to 425° F and preheat the oven. Grease a round baking dish with butter and keep it in the oven while preheating.

Add milk, eggs, vanilla, flour, sugar, and salt into a blender and blend until smooth.

Add the batter into the baking dish. Place the dish in the oven and set the timer for about 20 minutes or until it puffs up and golden brown around the edges.

Cool for 5 minutes. Cut into wedges. Serve with any one or more of the suggested serving options.

Banana Nut Bread

Serves: 8

Ingredients:

2 cups whole-wheat pastry flour

⅛ teaspoon salt

¾ cup brown sugar

2 eggs or flax eggs

4 over ripe bananas, mashed

2 teaspoons vanilla extract

4 tablespoon butter, melted

1 cup chopped walnuts

Directions:

If you want to make the bread vegan, use flax eggs. For this, whisk together tablespoon ground flaxseed with 3 tablespoons of water and place it in the refrigerator for 15 minutes. It will be gel-like. Also use vegan butter instead of regular butter.

Set the temperature of the oven to 375° F and preheat the oven. Grease a loaf pan with some cooking spray.

Add bananas, brown sugar, baking soda, and salt into a mixing bowl and whisk well, until very smooth.

Add eggs, vanilla extract, and butter and mix.

Add flour and fold until just combined. Do not over-mix.

Pour the batter into the loaf pan. You can use a baking dish if you do not have a loaf pan.

Sprinkle walnuts on top of the batter.

Put the loaf pan in the oven and set the timer for about 30–40 minutes or until cooked well inside. To check if it is done, insert a toothpick or knife in the center of the loaf. Remove it and check for any particles that may be stuck on it. If you find any particles, bake for some more time else, switch off the oven.

Remove the loaf pan from the oven and let it cool for a while. Invert onto a plate. Slice and serve.

Store leftover bread in an airtight container in the refrigerator. It can last for 8–9 days.

Instead of bread, you can make muffins with the same batter. You will have to bake for about 25 minutes if you want to make muffins.

Apple Honey Dutch Baby

Serves: 8

Ingredients:

6 large eggs, at room temperature

1 ½ cups all-purpose flour

4 tablespoons butter

1 ½ cups 2% milk

2 tablespoons sugar

For topping:

4 large apples, sliced

4–6 teaspoons lemon juice

2 teaspoons cornstarch mixed with 4 teaspoons cold water

2 tablespoons butter

1 cup honey

1 teaspoon ground cardamom

Directions:

Set the temperature of the oven to 400° F and preheat the oven. Place butter in a round baking dish and place it in the oven while preheating.

Beat eggs in a bowl. Add butter, milk, sugar, and flour and beat until smooth batter is formed.

Take out the baking dish and swirl it around so that the butter is spread all over the bottom and sides of the baking dish.

Spoon the batter into the baking dish and place it back in the oven. Set the timer for 18–22 minutes or until light brown around the edges.

To make topping: Add butter into a saucepan and place it over medium heat on your stovetop. When butter melts, add apples and cook until light brown.

Add lemon juice, honey, and cardamom and stir well.

Stir in the cornstarch mixture. Keep stirring until the mixture is thick and starts boiling.

Cut the pancake into wedges. Top with sauce and serve.

Chocolate Granola Bars

Serves: 15–16

Ingredients:

3 ½ cups old fashioned oats

2 tablespoons chia seeds

2 teaspoons ground cinnamon

1 cup natural peanut butter

1 cup unsweetened milk of your choice

4 tablespoons mini chocolate chips

1 cup vanilla or chocolate protein powder

2 tablespoons cocoa powder

½ teaspoon salt

1 cup maple syrup or honey or agave nectar

¼ cup chopped almonds

Sea salt to sprinkle

Directions:

Set the temperature of the oven to 350° F and preheat the oven. Prepare a baking dish of about 13 x 9 inches by greasing it with cooking spray.

Add peanut butter and maple syrup into a microwave safe bowl. Microwave on High for 30–40 seconds until well combined. Stir every 20 seconds.

Add all the dry ingredients into a mixing bowl, i.e. oats, chia seeds, cinnamon, protein powder, cocoa, and salt and stir. Add the peanut butter mixture and milk and mix until the mixture comes together like dough.

Transfer into the prepared baking dish.

Scatter almonds on top and press lightly so that they are slightly embedded in the mixture.

Place the baking dish in the oven and set the timer for 15 to 20 minutes or until slightly firm.

Take out the dish from the oven. Scatter chocolate chips on top. Press the chocolate chips lightly to adhere. Sprinkle salt all over the top.

Cut into 16 equal bars.

Transfer the bars into an airtight container and refrigerate until use. These bars can last for about 2 to 3 weeks.

Breakfast Bake

Serves: 3

Ingredients:

10 ounces refrigerated hash brown potatoes

½ tablespoon olive oil

⅛ teaspoon dried oregano

⅛ teaspoon dried basil

⅛ teaspoon dried thyme

⅛ teaspoon garlic powder

½ cup shredded cheddar cheese

3 large eggs

1 tablespoon chopped fresh chives

6 slices bacon

2 tablespoons freshly grated Parmesan cheese

Salt to taste

Freshly ground pepper to taste

1 tablespoon unsalted butter, melted

Directions:

Set the temperature of the oven to 400° F and preheat the oven.

Take a baking sheet or baking dish and grease it with cooking spray.

Place the hash browns in the dish. Add butter, herbs, garlic powder, salt, pepper, and oil and stir until well combined. Now spread it evenly.

Top with cheese and keep it in the oven. Set the timer for about 20 minutes or until light brown around the edges.

Make three cavities in the mixture, at different spots. Crack an egg into each cavity. Place bacon slices all over the top of the hash browns.

Put it back into the oven and set the timer for 10 to 12 minutes or until the eggs and bacon are cooked as per your preference.

Garnish with chives and serve.

Overnight Breakfast Strata

Serves: 6

Ingredients:

2.5 ounces seasoned croutons

¾ cup coarsely chopped cooked ham

3 ounces frozen chopped spinach, thawed, squeezed of excess moisture

5 medium eggs

¾ cup half and half

¼ teaspoon ground white pepper

2.5 ounces butter and garlic croutons or use regular croutons

2 ounces finely shredded cheddar cheese

3 ounces chopped, roasted red pepper from jar

¾ cup milk

Salt to taste

Directions:

Grease the baking dish by spraying with cooking spray.

Scatter croutons on the bottom of the dish. Scatter ham, red pepper, and spinach over the croutons.

Crack eggs into a bowl. Add salt, pepper, and half and half and beat until well combined.

Drizzle the egg mixture all over the croutons. Cover the baking dish with aluminum foil and place it in the refrigerator overnight.

Set the temperature of the oven to 350° F and preheat the oven.

Take out the baking dish from the refrigerator and place it in the oven.

Set the timer for about 45 minutes. Now remove the foil covering and bake for another 10 minutes.

Serve hot. You can store the leftovers in an airtight container in the refrigerator. Reheat the strata in an oven before serving.

Oatmeal Breakfast Bake

Serves: 4

Ingredients:

1 cup rolled oats

¼ cup peanut butter or any other nut butter or seed butter of your choice

¼ cup mixed berries of your choice

1 large banana, sliced

¼ teaspoon vanilla extract

2 tablespoons mix-ins of your choice (optional)

Directions:

Place a sheet of parchment paper on the bottom of a 5–6 inch square baking pan.

Set the temperature of the oven to 350° F and preheat the oven.

Add oats, peanut butter, banana and vanilla into a mixing bowl and mix until well combined.

Add mix-ins if using and half the berries and fold into the mixture.

Spoon the mixture into the prepared baking dish. Spread it evenly.

Scatter remaining berries on top. Press the berries lightly so that they are slightly embedded in the mixture.

Place the baking pan in the oven and set the timer for about 20 minutes or a knife when inserted in the center comes out clean, without any particles stuck on it when you pull it out.

Remove the baking pan from the oven and place on your countertop for 10 minutes. Remove and place on a wire rack. Let it cool to room temperature.

Cut into four equal portions and serve.

Cinnamon Rolls

Serves: 18

Ingredients:

5 ½ cups all-purpose flour

2 teaspoons salt

1 cup water

4 tablespoons unsalted butter

6 tablespoons granulated sugar

2 packages (1 ¼ teaspoons each) instant yeast

½ cup milk

2 large eggs

For the filling:

4 tablespoons ground cinnamon

½ cup unsalted butter, at room temperature

½ cup brown sugar

For the glaze:

2 teaspoons vanilla extract

2 cups powdered sugar

4–6 tablespoons milk

Directions:

Add salt, flour, sugar, and yeast into a mixing bowl and stir until well combined.

Add milk, butter, and water into a microwave safe container and place it in the microwave. Cook on high for about a minute or until butter melts and is warm, around 110° F.

Pour the milk mixture into the mixing bowl and mix well. Add eggs and mix well until you get dough. You can use your hands or fix the dough attachment in the stand mixer to knead the dough.

Knead until smooth. Grease a bowl with some oil. Take out the dough from the mixing bowl and keep it in the greased bowl.

Set aside for 5 minutes.

Set the temperature of the oven to 400° F and preheat the oven for just 10 minutes. Turn off the oven. Grease two large baking dishes (13 x 9 inches) with some cooking spray.

Divide the dough into two equal portions. Dust your countertop and the rolling pin with some flour.

Roll each portion into a rectangle of about 15 x 9 inches. Divide the butter equally and spread over the rolled dough.

Combine cinnamon and sugar in a bowl. Divide equally the cinnamon sugar and scatter all over the rolled dough.

Start rolling the dough tightly from one of the longer ends, right up to the other end. Roll the other dough similarly.

Cut each log into nine equal portions and keep them in the prepared baking dishes, upright (you should be able to see the cut part of each piece). Make sure to leave sufficient space between the rolls.

Now cover the baking dishes with cling wrap and place them in the oven. Do not turn on the oven as of now.

Let the rolls rest in the oven for 20 minutes. Now turn the oven on and turn down the temperature of the oven to 375° F.

Bake in batches, without covering. Set the timer for 20 minutes or until golden brown. Let them cool on your countertop for about 20 to 30 minutes or until warm.

To make glaze: Add powdered sugar, milk, and vanilla into a bowl and mix well. Trickle the glaze all over the rolls and serve.

Store leftover rolls in an airtight container in the refrigerator. Heat for a few seconds in the microwave if desired and serve. You can also serve at room temperature.

Pumpkin Pie Breakfast Cookies

Serves: 30

Ingredients:

1 cup pumpkin puree

½ cup honey or maple syrup

2 ½ cups quick oats

1 teaspoon baking powder

1 cup natural peanut butter

2 tablespoons vanilla extract

4 teaspoons pumpkin pie spice

Directions:

Set the temperature of the oven to 350° F and preheat the oven.

Prepare three baking sheets by lining them with parchment paper.

Add pumpkin puree, honey, peanut butter, and vanilla extract (you can melt the peanut butter in a microwave for a few seconds if it is not very soft) into a bowl and whisk well.

Add oats, baking powder, and pumpkin pie spice and stir until just incorporated.

Scoop with a cookie scoop, the mixture on the baking sheet. Flatten the cookies to the desired thickness. Leave sufficient gaps between the cookies as they will become bigger on baking.

Bake in batches for 12–15 minutes or until light golden brown around the edges.

Remove baking sheets from the oven and let the cookies cool for 7–8 minutes on the baking sheet. Loosen the cookies with a metal spatula.

Cool completely. Leftover cookies can be transferred into an airtight container and stored at room temperature for 3 days or in the freezer for 2 months. If you freeze them, thaw before serving.

Lunch

Pizza Burrito

Serves: 2

Ingredients:

For pizza sauce:

¼ cup tomato paste

¾ teaspoon dried basil

¾ teaspoon dried thyme

½ teaspoon dried oregano

½ teaspoon smoked paprika

½ teaspoon sea salt

¼ cup vegetable broth or water

½ teaspoon garlic powder

½ teaspoon maple syrup or sugar

For burrito pizza:

2 tortillas

½ cup sliced mushrooms

½ cup fresh packed spinach

3 tablespoons mayonnaise

¼ cup grated cheese of your choice

1 tablespoon chopped fresh basil to garnish

Directions:

Set the temperature of the oven to 350° F and preheat the oven. Prepare a square baking dish by lining it with parchment paper

To make pizza sauce: Add tomato paste, spices, broth, and maple syrup into a small bowl and stir.

To assemble: Warm the tortillas following the instructions on the package.

Spread pizza sauce on each tortilla.

Scatter half the spinach on each. Drizzle 1 ½ tablespoons mayonnaise on each and spread it.

Scatter half the mushrooms on each tortilla followed by half the cheese.

Fold like a burrito and place them in the baking dish.

Put the baking dish in the oven and set the timer for about 18–20 minutes or until crisp.

BBQ Flavored Baked Tofu

Serves: 2

Ingredients:

½ cup BBQ sauce

1 block (½ pound) firm tofu or extra-firm tofu, pressed of excess moisture

To serve:

Lettuce

Tomato slices

Pickle or relish

Any other toppings of your choice

Directions:

You need to press the tofu of excess moisture. For this, take out the tofu from the package and place it on a plate lined with paper towels. Place something heavy over the tofu like a cold drink can or heavy pan. Let it remain this way for at least 30 minutes. If you can keep it for 1 to 2 hours, that would be great.

Set the temperature of the oven to 325° F and preheat the oven.

Take a baking dish and spread a thin layer of BBQ sauce on the bottom of the dish.

Cut the tofu into ½ inch thick slices and place in the baking dish.

Spread a thin layer of BBQ sauce over the tofu.

Place the baking dish in the oven and set the timer for 20–25 minutes.

Serve with suggested serving options.

Roasted Salmon With Fennel Salad

Serves: 2

Ingredients:

1 teaspoon finely chopped fresh flat-leaf parsley

Salt to taste

1 tablespoon olive oil

⅓ cup reduced-fat, 2% Greek yogurt

1 tablespoon fresh orange juice

1 tablespoon chopped fresh dill

½ teaspoon minced fresh thyme

2 salmon filets, skinless, center-cut

2 cups thinly sliced fennel

2 small cloves garlic, peeled, grated

½ teaspoon fresh lemon juice

Directions:

Set the temperature of the oven to 400° F and preheat the oven.

Add salt and herbs in a bowl and mix well.

Brush oil over the salmon. Scatter the herb mixture over it and place in a baking dish.

Place the baking dish in the oven and set the timer for 12–15 minutes or until cooked through. It should flake when you pierce it with a fork.

Meanwhile, combine fennel, yogurt, orange juice, garlic, lemon juice, and salt in a bowl and stir until well combined.

Divide fennel salad into two plates. Place salmon filets on top and serve.

Greek Salad Chicken Wrap

Serves: 4

Ingredients:

For chicken:

4 bone-in chicken breasts

2 teaspoons dried oregano

2 teaspoons lemon pepper or to taste

2 teaspoons garlic powder or more to taste

2 tablespoons olive oil

For salad:

8 cups chopped romaine lettuce

½ cup chopped red onion

¼ cup pitted, sliced kalamata olives

⅔ cup sliced cherry tomatoes

1 medium cucumber, cut into half-moon slices

⅔ cup feta cheese

Pepper to taste

Olive oil to drizzle

Red wine vinegar to drizzle

½ teaspoon dried oregano or to taste

2 tablespoons lemon juice or to taste

Salt to taste

To assemble:

4 whole-wheat or gluten-free wraps

8 tablespoons hummus

Directions:

For chicken: Set the temperature of the oven to 375° F and preheat the oven.

Place a sheet of foil on the bottom of a baking dish. Spray some cooking spray over the foil.

Sprinkle salt, pepper, lemon pepper, and dried oregano over the chicken breasts and place them in the baking dish.

Drizzle remaining oil over the chicken.

Place the baking dish in the oven and set the timer for about 40 minutes or until the chicken is cooked through. When cool enough to handle, slice the chicken.

Meanwhile, add lettuce, onion, olives, tomatoes, cucumber, feta, oregano, lemon juice, salt, and pepper into a bowl and toss well. Drizzle some vinegar and oil and toss well.

To assemble: Place the wraps on your countertop. Smear 2 tablespoons of hummus on each wrap. Place chicken slices over the wraps. Divide the salad among the wraps.

Fold like a burrito and serve.

Baked Chicken Taquitos

Serves: 4

Ingredients:

2 cups shredded cooked chicken breast

4 tablespoons taco sauce

8 corn tortillas (6 inches each)

½ cup shredded low-fat cheddar cheese

1 teaspoon ground cumin

Directions:

Set the temperature of the oven to 425° F and preheat the oven.

Prepare a baking sheet by lining it with parchment paper.

To make filling: Add chicken, taco sauce, chicken and cumin in a bowl and mix until well combined.

Warm up the tortillas following the directions given on the package of tortillas.

Divide the chicken filling among the tortillas and place near any one of the sides of the tortilla. Roll each and place it on the baking sheet.

Place the baking sheet in the oven and set the timer for about 15 minutes or bake until light brown on the edges.

Sweet Potato and Crispy Kale Tostadas

Serves: 1–2

Ingredients:

1 medium sweet potato, scrubbed, chopped into cubes

Cayenne pepper to taste

1 ½ tablespoons olive oil, divided

6 Brussels sprouts, finely chopped

½ teaspoon honey

Yogurt, to drizzle

1 tablespoon chopped mint (optional)

4 kale leaves, chopped, discard hard stem and ribs

Salt to taste

½ tablespoon lime juice

Corn tortillas, as required

1–2 tablespoons toasted, shredded coconut (optional)

Directions:

Set the temperature of the oven to 350° F and preheat the oven.

Line a baking dish with foil. Place sweet potato in the dish. Drizzle half the oil over it. Sprinkle cayenne pepper over the sweet potato.

Take another baking dish and line it with foil. Place kale in the dish. Drizzle remaining oil over the kale. Sprinkle salt and toss well. Place both the baking dishes in the oven. Set the timer for about 20–30 minutes or until sweet potatoes are tender.

Take out the kale after about 8–10 minutes of baking or whenever it turns crisp on the edges. Do not bake the kale for long as the kale can get burnt.

Place Brussels sprouts in a bowl. Drizzle lime juice and honey over it. Toss well.

Warm the tortillas following the instructions given on the package of the tortillas.

To assemble the tostadas: Place tortillas on a serving platter. Divide the sweet potato and kale among the tortillas.

Place Brussels sprouts over the sweet potatoes. Drizzle some yogurt. Sprinkle mint and shredded coconut if using and serve.

Dinner

Salsa Chicken

Serves: 3

Ingredients:

1 cup salsa

½ ounces low-sodium taco seasoning

¼ cup low-fat sharp cheddar cheese

¼ cup sour cream preferably nonfat

¾ pound chicken breasts, skinless, boneless

Cilantro or sliced green onions to garnish

Directions:

Set the temperature of the oven to 350° F and preheat the oven.

Grease a small baking dish with cooking spray.

Add sour cream, salsa, and taco seasoning into a bowl and mix well.

Place chicken in the baking dish. Spread some salsa on the bottom of the dish. Place chicken in the dish. Spread remaining salsa over the chicken.

Place the baking dish in the oven and set the timer for about 30–40 minutes or until cooked through.

Garnish with cilantro and cheese and serve.

Creamy Pesto Chicken

Serves: 4

Ingredients:

<u>For the chicken:</u>

2 tablespoons balsamic vinegar

2 teaspoons dried oregano

½ teaspoon salt or to taste

2 teaspoons olive oil

1 teaspoon minced garlic

4 boneless, skinless, chicken breast halves (6 ounces each)

<u>For pesto:</u>

½ cup packed fresh parsley leaves

½ cup loosely packed basil leaves

½ cup canned coconut milk

½ teaspoon salt

Directions:

Set the temperature of the oven to 350° F and preheat the oven. Prepare a baking dish by greasing it with cooking spray.

To make chicken: Combine balsamic vinegar, oregano, salt, olive oil, and garlic in a bowl. Brush this mixture over the chicken and place the chicken in the baking dish.

To make pesto: Blend together basil, salt and parsley in the food processor until finely chopped.

With the blender machine running, pour coconut milk through the feeder tube in a thin drizzle and process until smooth and well combined.

Divide chicken into serving plates and serve with pesto.

Baked Tilapia With Pecan Rosemary Topping

Serves: 2

Ingredients:

3 tablespoons chopped raw pecans

1 teaspoon chopped fresh rosemary

Salt to taste

1 teaspoon olive oil

2 tilapia filets (4 ounces each)

3 tablespoons whole-wheat panko breadcrumbs or regular breadcrumbs

1 teaspoon coconut palm sugar or brown sugar

Cayenne pepper to taste

1 egg, beaten

Directions:

Set the temperature of the oven to 350° F and preheat the oven.

Add pecans, rosemary, salt, breadcrumbs, sugar and cayenne pepper into a small baking dish and stir well.

Stir in the oil. Once the oil is well combined, spread it evenly and place it in the oven.

Set the timer for about 7–8 minutes or until light golden brown in color. Remove the dish from the oven.

Raise the temperature of the oven to 400° F. Grease the baking dish with some oil.

Working with one fish filet at a time, dip a filet in egg. Shake to drop off excess egg. Next dredge in pecan mixture. Shake to drop off excess pecan mixture and place the filet in the baking dish.

Sprinkle remaining pecan mixture over the filets. Press lightly to adhere. Place the baking dish in the oven.

Set the timer for about 10 minutes or until filets are cooked.

Texas BBQ Brisket

Serves: 5

Ingredients:

1 tablespoon packed brown sugar

½ tablespoon onion powder

½ tablespoon ground mustard

½ tablespoon pepper

½ tablespoon salt

½ tablespoon garlic powder

½ tablespoon smoked paprika

1 fresh beef brisket (about 3 ½ pounds), pricked all over with a sharp knife

¼ cup liquid smoke

½ bottle (from a 10 ounce bottle) Heinz steak sauce

⅛ cup Worcestershire sauce

Directions:

Add brown sugar, onion powder, mustard, pepper, salt, garlic powder, and paprika into a bowl and stir until well combined.

Sprinkle the spice mixture all over the brisket and rub it well into it using your hands. Place it in a bowl. Cover and keep it in the refrigerator for 8–9 hours.

Set the temperature of the oven to 325° F and preheat the oven.

Add steak sauce, Worcestershire sauce, and liquid smoke into a bowl and mix well.

Put the steak in a roasting pan, with the fat side facing on top. Drizzle the sauce mixture all over the brisket.

Cover the meat along with the roasting pan with aluminum foil. Place it in the oven and bake until tender. It will take a few hours to cook, about 3–4 hours.

Once the meat is tender, let it rest for 15 minutes in the roasting pan itself.

Take out the meat from the roasting pan and place on your cutting board.

When cool enough to handle, cut into thin slices across the grain.

Remove any fat that is floating on top of the cooked liquids in the roasting pan.

Serve meat slices on serving plates. Pour cooked juices on top and serve.

Ribs With Plum Sauce

Serves: 3

Ingredients:

2 ½ – 3 pounds pork spareribs, cut into serving size pieces

6–7 tablespoons plum jam or apricot preserves

1 large clove garlic, peeled, minced

6 tablespoons low-sodium soy sauce

6 tablespoons honey

Directions:

Set the temperature of the oven to 350° F and preheat the oven.

Place the spare ribs in a roasting pan, with the bone side facing down.

Cover the roasting pan tightly with foil and place it in the oven.

Set the timer for about 50–60 minutes or until tender. Remove the foil covering and discard.

Add plum jam, garlic, soy sauce, and honey into a bowl and stir until smooth.

Brush this mixture over the meat and continue baking for about 25–30 minutes, basting with the sauce every 10 minutes. As you baste, turn the meat over.

Roast Rack of Lamb With Herb Sauce

Serves: 2

Ingredients:

⅛ cup minced fresh rosemary

Salt to taste

½ tablespoon olive oil

Coarsely ground pepper to taste

1 rack of lamb (1 ½ pounds)

For the sauce:

⅓ cup fresh basil leaves

½ cup parsley leaves

3 tablespoons fresh cilantro leaves

3 tablespoons fresh mint leaves

3 tablespoons fresh oregano leaves

3 tablespoons fresh thyme leaves

3 tablespoons fresh chopped chives

1 clove garlic, crushed

¼ cup lemon juice

Salt to taste

3 tablespoons olive oil

3 tablespoons chopped shallots

1 ½ tablespoons grated lemon zest

1 tablespoon Dijon mustard

¼ teaspoon pepper

Directions:

Add pepper, rosemary, and salt into a bowl and mix well. Rub this mixture all over the lamb. Keep it in a bowl and cover with cling wrap. Place the bowl in the refrigerator for 8–10 hours.

Set the temperature of the oven to 375° F and preheat the oven.

Take out the lamb from the refrigerator and keep it in a roasting pan, with the fat side on top.

Trickle oil over the lamb and put it into the oven. Set the timer for about 45 minutes or cook as per your preference i.e. 135° F for medium-rare or 140° F for medium or 145° F for medium-well cooked.

Once it is cooked as per your preference, take it out from the oven and cover it loosely with foil. Let it rest for 10 minutes.

Add shallots, all the fresh herbs and garlic into the food process bowl and process until finely chopped.

Add lemon juice, lemon zest, salt, mustard, and pepper and process until well combined. With the food processor machine running, pour oil in a drizzle through the feeder tube. Process until well combined.

Cut lamb int0 pieces. Pour sauce on top and serve.

Tofu and Winter Squash Lasagna

Serves: 2–3

Ingredients:

½ pound no boil lasagna noodles

½ tablespoon packed brown sugar

¼ cup milk of your choice

Pepper to taste

½ tablespoon chopped fresh leaves

Salt to taste

Seasoned bread or cracker crumbs (optional)

1 cup cooked, mashed winter squash or acorn squash or butternut squash

½ pound soft tofu

1 tablespoon fresh lemon juice

⅛ teaspoon smoked paprika

2 cups marinara sauce

Directions:

Set the temperature of the oven to 350° F and preheat the oven.

Add squash and brown sugar into a bowl and mix well.

Add tofu, lemon juice, paprika, milk, thyme, salt, pepper and paprika into the food processor bowl and process until well incorporated.

Transfer the blended mixture into the bowl of squash and mix well.

Take a baking dish for about 8–9 inches. Spread a thin layer of the marinara sauce on the bottom of the baking dish.

Place a layer of noodles. Spread some of the squash mixture over the noodles.

Repeat layering of sauce, noodles and squash mixture until the ingredients are used up.

Finally sprinkle bread crumbs if using.

Place the baking dish and set the timer for about 30–40 minutes or until golden brown on top.

Dessert

Apple Cranberry Cobbler

Serves: 4

Ingredients:

4 small apples like Granny Smith, Honey crisp etc., cored, cut into thin wedges

2 tablespoons honey or sugar

2 teaspoons vanilla extract

½ teaspoon ground nutmeg

4 tablespoons dried cranberries

2 tablespoons water

1 teaspoon ground cinnamon

4 tablespoons low fat granola, without raisins

Olive oil cooking spray

Directions:

Set the temperature of the oven to 350° F and preheat the oven.

Grease a baking dish with some cooking spray.

Combine apple slices, honey, vanilla, cranberries, water, and spices in a large bowl. Toss well.

Place the apple slices in concentric circles in the baking dish, slightly overlapping. Keep the baking dish covered with foil.

Place it in the oven and set the timer for about 20–25 minutes or until the apples are cooked.

Remove the foil and discard it. Sprinkle granola on top. Continue baking for another 5 minutes or until brown on top.

Spiced Chocolate Molten Cakes

Serves: 4

Ingredients:

½ cup butter, cut into cubes

3 teaspoons dry red wine

2 large eggs, at room temperature

1 cup confectioners' sugar + extra to top

¼ teaspoon ground ginger

4 ounces semi-sweet chocolate, chopped

1 teaspoon vanilla extract

2 egg yolks, at room temperature

6 tablespoons all-purpose flour

¼ teaspoon ground cinnamon

Directions:

Set the temperature of the oven to 425° F and preheat the oven.

Add chocolate and butter into a microwave safe bowl and cook on High for about a minute or until smooth. Stir every 20 seconds.

Add vanilla and wine and stir until well combined.

Crack eggs into a bowl. Add confectioners' sugar and yolks and beat until thick.

Add ginger, flour, and cinnamon and beat until well combined.

Beat in the chocolate mixture, a little at a time.

Grease four small baking dishes or ramekins (about 6–8 ounces each) with some cooking spray and place them on a baking sheet.

Divide equally and pour the batter into the ramekins. Place the baking sheet in the oven and set the timer for 12 minutes or until a thermometer when placed in the center of the cake shows 160° F on the thermometer.

Let the cakes cool for a minute. Loosen the cakes by running a knife around the edges of the cake.

Serve with some confectioners' sugar sprinkled on top.

Cranberry Apple Lattice Pie

Serves: 4

Ingredients:

1 ¼ cups all-purpose flour

⅓ teaspoon salt

3 tablespoons cold shortening

½ tablespoon sugar

¼ cup cold unsalted butter, cut into cubes

2–3 tablespoons ice water

For the filling:

1 tablespoon dark rum or water

6 tablespoons sugar, divided

1 tablespoon quick-cooking tapioca

1 teaspoon grated lemon zest

¼ cup dried currants or raisins

½ cup fresh or frozen cranberries, divided

3 medium baking apples like Fuji (about 1 pound), peeled, cored, cut into ¼ inch thick slices

½ tablespoon fresh lemon juice

¼ teaspoon ground cinnamon

For the egg wash:

A pinch ground cinnamon

½ tablespoon milk or heavy whipping cream

1 teaspoon sugar

1 small egg

Directions:

Combine flour, salt and sugar in a bowl. Add butter and shortening and cut it into the flour mixture until you get crumbs.

Pour water and stir with a fork until the mixture sticks together when you press some of it.

Make two equal portions of the mixture and shape into balls. Now flatten the balls into thick, round discs.

Wrap each in cling wrap and chill for at least 30 minutes.

Meanwhile, place currants in a bowl. Pour rum over it and let it soak for 20 minutes.

Add ⅓ cup cranberries and 2 tablespoons sugar into the food processor bowl and give short pulses until cranberries are chopped.

Remove the cranberries into a bowl. Stir in apples, lemon zest, 4 tablespoons sugar, tapioca, cinnamon, lemon juice, and soaked currants along with rum. Let it rest for 15 minutes.

Set the temperature of the oven to 400° F and preheat the oven.

Dust your countertop with a little flour. Take one disc of dough and roll into a round of about ⅛ inch thick.

Lift the dough and place it in a small deep dish pie pan. The edges of the rolled dough should slightly overhang from the edges of the pie pan.

Spread the filling over the dough in the pie pan.

Now again dust your countertop with a little flour and roll the other dough disc into a round of about ⅛ inch thick.

With a sharp knife, cut out strips about ½ inch wide.

Place the strips in a lattice pattern over the filling. Trim the edges of the crust if necessary.

Drop the remaining cranberries in the holes of the lattice pattern.

Beat egg in a bowl adding milk. Combine cinnamon and sugar in another bowl.

Brush egg mixture on top of the lattice strips. Scatter cinnamon sugar over the strips.

Place it on the lower rack in the oven. Set the timer for 20 minutes. Now turn down the temperature of the oven to 325° F and continue baking until the crust turns golden brown and the filling is bubbling away.

Once baked, take it out from the oven and place it on a wire rack.

Cut into wedges once it cools slightly and serve.

Jumbo Brownie Cookies

Serves: 8–9

Ingredients:

1 ⅓ cups 60% bitter-sweet chocolate chips

2 large eggs, at room temperature

2 teaspoons vanilla extract

⅓ cup all-purpose flour

⅛ teaspoon salt

¼ cup unsalted butter, cut into cubes

¾ cup sugar

1 teaspoon instant espresso powder (optional)

¼ teaspoon baking powder

½ package (from a 11 ½ ounces package) semi-sweet chocolate chunks

Directions:

Set the temperature of the oven to 400° F and preheat the oven.

Place chocolate chips and butter in a microwave safe bowl and place it in the microwave. Cook on high for about a minute or until the mixture melts and is smooth. Stir every 20 seconds.

Let the mixture cool until it is warm.

Meanwhile, crack eggs into a bowl. Add vanilla, espresso powder, and sugar and whisk until smooth.

Pour into the melted chocolate and whisk well.

Combine all the dry ingredients in another bowl, i.e. flour, salt, and baking powder.

Add the mixture of dry ingredients into the bowl of chocolate mixture and stir until smooth.

Add chocolate chunks and fold gently. Let the batter rest for about 10 minutes.

Line a large baking sheet with parchment paper.

Scoop out about ¼ cup of the batter and drop it on the baking sheet. Leave sufficient gaps between the cookies.

Place the baking sheet in the oven and set the timer for 12–14 minutes or until cooked around the edges.

Take out the baking sheet and let the cookies cool on the baking sheet for a couple of minutes.

Loosen the cookies with a metal spatula. Place them on a cooling rack.

Cool completely and serve. Leftover cookies can be transferred into an airtight container and stored at room temperature for 3 days or in the freezer for 2 months. If you freeze them, thaw before serving.

Honey Roasted Cashews

Serves: 8

Ingredients:

½ pound lightly salted cashews

1 tablespoon pure maple syrup

A pinch kosher salt

⅛ teaspoon ground cinnamon

1 tablespoon honey

1 tablespoon unsalted butter

½ teaspoon vanilla extract

2 tablespoons raw sugar or coconut sugar

Directions:

Set the temperature of the oven to 350° F and preheat the oven.

Combine maple syrup, honey and butter in a small pan.

Place the pan over heat. Stir until butter melts and the mixture is well incorporated. Turn off the heat.

Add vanilla extract and cinnamon and whisk well. Add cashews and stir until the cashews are well coated.

Transfer onto a baking sheet and spread it evenly, without overlapping.

Place the baking sheet in the oven and set the timer for about 18 minutes.

Stir the cashews every 6 minutes and spread it each time you stir.

Once roasted, transfer the cashews into a bowl. Add sugar and salt and stir until well coated with sugar and salt.

Line the baking sheet with parchment paper and spread the cashews on the baking sheet.

Once the cashews are completely cooled, transfer into an airtight container and store at room temperature until use.

Conclusion

Paying attention to nutrition is needed. Healthy food seems to be all the rage these days. Walk into any supermarket and you will be surrounded by different food products claiming to be healthy in one form or another. However, instead of spending a significant portion of your food budget on it, what if you could cook all these at home? Cooking healthy meals doesn't mean spending hours together in the kitchen or hundreds of your hardened dollars on expensive and exotic ingredients. Instead, it's about learning to do the most with whatever you have on hand. This is what frugal meals are all about. With a little meal planning, preparation as well as batch cooking, cooking itself becomes a breeze. In this book, you'll not only learn how to eat healthier on a budget but reduce wastage of food and understand zero-waste cooking at home.

Most of us use different appliances, utensils, and equipment when it comes to cooking. Even if you find the act of cooking enjoyable and relaxing, all the prep involved before and cleaning up after it is seldom fun. However, you don't have to worry about all this once you are armed with the different recipes you were introduced to in this book. This book will introduce you to a world of healthy and tasty recipes that can be cooked within no time using a single pot! Cooking doesn't get any easier than this. Whether it is breakfast, lunch, dinner, or even a dessert, everything can be cooked in a single pot. All it requires is a little creativity and the good news is that you needn't spend any additional time searching for recipes that fit all these requirements.

When it comes to cooking, one of the most important things you must remember is that eating healthy beers is not anonymous to consuming meals that are bland and boring. It also doesn't mean you need to splurge and burn a hole in your pocket trying to eat healthily. You can cook delicious simple and healthy meals while sticking to a fixed budget. This is also a process that doesn't involve multiple pots and pans. Instead, cooking is possible with a single pot. Whether it's a sauté pan, slow cooker or instant pot, or baking dish, you simply need a little creativity. Before you get started, take some time, and make a meal plan by yourself. You simply need to make a list of different recipes that strike your fancy. Once all the recipes are in place, look for any overlapping ingredients or cooked components. This is the best way of implementing a zero-wastage policy while cooking and eating at home. Once all this is in place, a little meal preparation and batch cooking will considerably cut down on the time spent in the kitchen. All this coupled with the fact that you will only be using a single pot to cook further reduces the time spent in the kitchen. By following the different recipes given in this book, you can easily stick to a strict food budget and improve your overall health.

Now that you have all the tools needed it's time to go ahead and start using them. The key to your health lies in your hands. You also have complete control over regulating your food budget. Before you go, I have a small favor to ask of you. If you enjoyed this book and the recipes given in it, can you please spare a few minutes to leave a review on Amazon?

Thank you and all the best!

References

Benefits of one-pot meals. (2020, August 24). The Wishing Well OT. https://www.thewishingwellot.com/blog/one-pot-meals

Bryan, L. (2019, September 17). 10 easy tips to eat healthy on a budget. Downshiftology. Https://downshiftology.com/healthy-eating-on-a-budget/

How long does food last in the freezer? (2021, November 12). Old Farmer's Almanac. https://www.almanac.com/content/freezer-storage-times-how-long-can-you-freeze-foods

Snyder, C. (2021, May 31). What is zero-waste cooking, and how do you do it? Healthline. https://www.healthline.com/nutrition/zero-waste-cooking-eating#tips

Image References

Bicker, D. (2021, October 17). Minestrone. Pixabay. https://pixabay.com/photos/minestrone-soup-minestrone-6714901/

Brouw, A. (2019, October 3). Tray of Cookies [Photograph]. Pexels. https://www.pexels.com/photo/tray-of-cookies-3065512/

Catkin. (2014, October 13). Rice pudding. Pixabay. https://pixabay.com/photos/rice-pudding-rice-cute-sweet-dish-480823/

Cirillo, V. (2018, August 12). American meatloaf. Pixabay. https://pixabay.com/photos/meatloaf-italian-cuisine-3599882/

Couleur. (2016, July 7). Chicken noodle soup. Pixabay. https://pixabay.com/photos/soup-beef-soup-noodle-soup-1503117/

Hourlay, D. (2015, February 27). Close-up Photography of Cocoa Powder [Photograph]. Pexels. https://www.pexels.com/photo/close-up-photography-of-cocoa-powder-691152/

JLerche. (2020, November 24). Crepes. Pixabay. https://pixabay.com/photos/crepes-blueberries-plate-breakfast-5767779/

NadiiaArt. (2021, December 3). Cinnamon rolls. Pixabay. https://pixabay.com/photos/apple-butter-rolls-6835925/

RitaE. (2018, July 19). Spaghetti. Pixabay. https://pixabay.com/photos/pasta-italian-cuisine-dish-3547078/

Suppenkasper. (2011, October 24). Pumpkin soup. Pixabay. https://pixabay.com/photos/pumpkin-soup-soup-orange-plate-10206/

Walter, D. (2019, January 16). Cauliflower soup. Pixabay. https://pixabay.com/photos/soup-cream-of-cauliflower-3930288/

Frank, Zhang (2021, February 1). https://unsplash.com/photos/iIpkL5kMLF0

WikimediaImages. (2017, April 4). Granola. Pixabay. https://pixabay.com/photos/food-eat-diet-chewy-granola-bar-2202344/

Printed in Great Britain
by Amazon

87119776R00086